CREATIVE COOKING COLLECTION

Cake Decorating

Cake Decorating

Janice Murfitt

CONTENTS

Simple Cake Decorating

Equipment	6
Decorations	7
Piping techniques	12
Basic cake mixtures	14
Simple icings	16
Small cakes	18
Decorated sponge cakes	24
Gâteaux	30

Elaborate Cake Decorating

Equipment	40
Basic cake mixtures	42
Marzipan, icings and piping	45
Designing the cake	54
Decorations	56
Celebration cakes	60
Index	80

Published exclusively for Cupress (Canada) Limited
10 Falconer Drive, Unit 8, Mississauga,
Ontario L5N 1B1, Canada
by Woodhead-Faulkner Ltd

First published 1987
© Woodhead-Faulkner (Publishers) Ltd 1987
ISBN 0-920691-28-5
Printed and bound in Italy by Arnoldo Mondadori Editore

INTRODUCTION

Cake decorating is often regarded as a hobby by those who enjoy it. Yet the thought of decorating a special occasion cake is a daunting prospect for many people. If you approach the task with confidence and patience, however, it is possible to achieve a very satisfying and rewarding result.

Being a complex subject, the art of cake decorating really needs to be mastered in stages. This book will show you stage by stage how to progress from a simply decorated sponge to an elaborate wedding cake.

The first and most important step is to make a cake worthy of icing. Basic recipes are given for delicious sponges and fruit cakes, including a light fruit cake for those who prefer something lighter than the traditional rich fruit cake.

The first section includes basic icings and simple decorations, and shows how a basic cake mixture can be made into a variety of cakes—large and small—with attractive finishes. Instructions for the use of nylon piping bags, parchment paper piping bags and simple nozzles are provided. A selection of irresistible gâteaux rounds off this section.

The second section takes you through the art of elaborate cake decorating. Basic recipes are provided for making marzipan, royal icing, and moulding icing. Step-by-step instructions show you how to apply them, and how to pipe intricate designs. There are also plenty of ideas for making your own decorations from marzipan and icing, to apply the finishing touches to celebration cakes.

To complete the section are recipes for all kinds of special occasion cakes, including a simple wedding cake which can be made during a weekend.

With patience and practice, you will be able to produce cakes that will be admired by everyone at special occasions.

NOTES

Ingredients are given in both metric and imperial measures. Use either set of quantities but not a mixture of both in any one recipe.

All spoon measurements are level:
1 tablespoon = one 15 ml spoon
1 teaspoon = one 5 ml spoon.

Ovens should be preheated to the temperature specified.

Eggs are large size unless otherwise stated.

SIMPLE CAKE DECORATING

EQUIPMENT

A selection of basic equipment is essential for cake icing and decorating, otherwise good results are difficult to obtain. General equipment should include a large and a small palette knife with flexible blade, spatula, wooden spoon, sieve, whisk and measuring cup. In addition you will need the items listed below. As you progress, add to your collection of icing equipment (see page 40).

Cups. All ingredients must be carefully measured to achieve perfect cakes.

Pans and moulds. Always choose good quality as the thickness of the metal is important; it ensures that cakes keep their shape, and also prevents overcooking or warping in the oven. The most popular sizes are 18–20 cm (7–8 inch) round and square, deep and shallow pans. Other sizes, not used so frequently, can always be rented from a kitchen shop when required.

Papers. Non-stick parchment paper and waxed papers all have their uses: waxed paper and parchment paper for lining pans; parchment paper for meringues, drying moulded or cut-out sugar decorations; waxed paper, which is fine and flexible, for run-outs.

Cutters. Sets of round cutters, plain and fluted, are always useful. Fancy cookie cutters will come in handy, too.

Glazing brushes. Small and large for brushing cake pans with melted fat or oil, and a large size for brushing cakes with glaze.

Ruler, scissors and pencil. Essential for cake decorating.

Turntable. This is the most essential piece of equipment. Although expensive, it will last for ever. Obtainable from most kitchen shops.

Piping bags. These are made in a variety of materials. The nylon ones are soft and flexible, perfect for cream, meringue and simple icing. Buy small, medium and large bags as these can be fitted with various-sized nozzles.

Nozzles. For simple piping, buy a selection of the smaller star and plain meringue nozzles. They are ideal for piping small cakes, and for decorating large cakes and gâteaux.

SIMPLE DECORATIONS

Here are a few ideas for effortless but effective cake decorations.

- Sweets, e.g. chocolate buttons, beans and sticks, jellies and liquorice allsorts, can be used for simple finishes.
- Ready-made sugar flowers, jelly diamonds and crystal-lized flower petals make attractive decorations.
- Orange, lemon and lime peel, angelica and cherries can be cut in inventive ways, using tiny cutters or a small, sharp knife, for a quick design on the cake.
- Hundreds and thousands, coloured dragees, mimosa balls and sugar strands make quick and colourful coatings, toppings and designs.

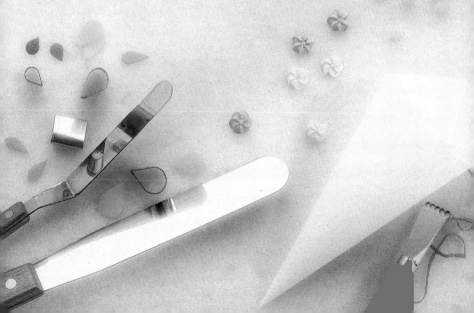

CHOCOLATE DECORATIONS

Chocolate can be melted down and used to make a variety of decorations. Milk, plain and white chocolate are all suitable.

To melt chocolate

1. Break the chocolate into small pieces and place in a clean, dry, heatproof bowl over a saucepan of hot—but not boiling—water, so that the base of the bowl is not touching the water. Only stir the chocolate occasionally.

2. When the chocolate has melted, remove bowl from heat and use as required. Do not overheat or allow water to get into the chocolate or it will harden instead of melting.

3. If the chocolate begins to set during use, scrape it down into the bowl and replace over the saucepan until melted.

Chocolate curls

1. Pour the melted chocolate onto a large chopping board, and spread quickly and evenly to the edges.

2. Leave the chocolate until just set but still soft enough to curl. Hard set chocolate is too brittle.

3. Place a long-bladed, sharp knife on the chocolate at the far side of the board and pull it towards you with the blade tilting backwards so that it shaves off a very fine curl of chocolate. Stop when the curl is large enough.

4. If the chocolate is too soft to curl, leave it for a few minutes. If it is too hard, leave it in a warm place for a few minutes, then try again.

5. For tiny curls, use a block of chocolate and a vegetable peeler to shave off small curls.

Chocolate cut-outs

1. Line a baking sheet with foil.
2. Pour the melted chocolate over the foil and spread quickly and evenly to the edges. Tap the baking sheet to level the chocolate, then leave for about 10 minutes, until just set but not brittle.
3. Use a long-bladed knife, dipped into hot water and dried, and a ruler to cut the chocolate into squares. Or use plain and fluted cutters to cut out shapes.

Piped chocolate pieces

1. Draw the required design as many times as needed on a piece of parchment or waxed paper.
2. Use a parchment paper piping bag (see page 12) fitted with a No. 1 plain writing nozzle, or just snip off a tiny point from the end. Half-fill the bag with melted chocolate and fold down the top. Squeeze very gently as chocolate flows quickly and pipe a thread of chocolate to cover each marked design.
3. Leave to set hard. Carefully remove each piece from the paper as required.

Chocolate leaves

1. Use fresh, dry rose leaves, with small stems if possible.
2. Using melted chocolate and a paintbrush, carefully coat the underside of each leaf evenly with chocolate, taking care not to get any chocolate on the tops of the leaves.
3. Place the leaves on a piece of parchment paper, chocolate side uppermost, in a cool place, but not in the refrigerator, to set hard.
4. When required, carefully peel the rose leaves away from the chocolate leaves.

SUGAR-FROSTED FLOWERS

If you have a little time, make your own decorations. These pretty flowers are simple to make, look most attractive and are edible. They can be made well in advance and stored in a warm dry place for several months. Choose simple, small flowers, such as primroses or violets, or frost the petals and leaves of slightly larger flowers separately. Rose petals are especially attractive.

1. Ensure the flowers are fresh and dry. Trim stems to required length. Pull the petals apart if you wish to frost them separately.
2. Using a fine paintbrush, paint each petal on both sides with lightly beaten egg white.
3. Brush the centre and stem with egg white, then carefully spoon over fine sugar to coat evenly.
4. Place on a wire rack covered with paper towels and leave in a warm dry place until the flowers are completely dry and set hard.
5. Store in an airtight container lined with paper towels for up to 3 months.

NOTE: Small leaves can be frosted in the same way. Herb leaves, such as mint, are particularly good.

COLOURS AND TINTS

Food colourings have changed over the last few years and almost any colour or shade can be obtained now. Always remember that a cake should look edible, so keep to pastel shades—a hint of colour is better than too much.

The food colourings commonly available in supermarkets and shops will readily tint or colour icings, frostings, butter creams, marzipan and moulding icing in the basic primary colours, and with careful blending can be used to produce other colours and shades.

Celebration cakes may require more subtle shading and tinting and most shades are now available from specialist shops. Moulded and cut-out flowers, and run-out pieces can be coloured with blossom tints, or painted with lustre colours, available in powder form, when they are dry. Painting helps to retain their colour, without fading, and also prevents the risk of colours running into the icing if the atmosphere is damp.

Food colourings are very concentrated and need to be used in tiny amounts. They are best added drop by drop, using a skewer. Colours deepen on standing and dry a darker shade than when first mixed. It is therefore best to colour icings in the daylight and leave for at least 15 minutes to assess the right colour.

If several batches of coloured icing have to be made, always keep some icing in reserve to match the colour.

PIPING BAGS AND SIMPLE TECHNIQUES

For piping butter icing, crème au beurre and whipped cream onto cakes and gâteaux, a nylon piping bag and meringue nozzles are the easiest to use, especially if you are a beginner. For piping glacé icing, melted chocolate, royal icing and simple butter icing designs, parchment paper piping bags are most suitable; these are quite easy to make yourself.

To Make a Parchment Paper Piping Bag

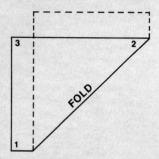

Cut out a rectangle of parchment paper 38 × 25 cm (15 × 10 inches). Fold diagonally into 2 equal pieces. Cut along fold.

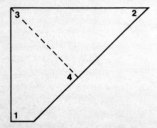

Take 1 piece of paper and number the points 1, 3 and 2. Fold in half to make a centre crease, open out flat again and number point 4.

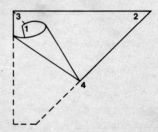

Place your finger on point 4 and turn point 1 with the thumb and finger until it is in line with point 3.

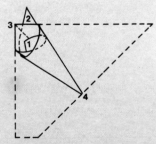

Holding point 1 in position, wrap point 2 round the cone and behind point 3. Pull tightly so the cone forms a sharp point at 4. Secure top of piping bag with sticky tape.

Using a Parchment Paper Piping Bag

To pipe a fine line, half-fill the bag with icing glacé and fold down the top. Snip a tiny piece off the end of the point until the desired line thickness is made.

For a leaf design, half-fill the bag with icing and fold down the top. Flatten the point and make 2 diagonal cuts that will cross in the centre to form a 'V'.

Using a Nylon Piping Bag

Choose the nozzle you require and fit it snugly into the bag so that there are no gaps. Half-fill the bag with icing or cream—over-filling the bag will make it difficult to handle. Twist the top of the bag until the mixture is forced to the end of the nozzle. Use one hand to position the nozzle just above the surface of the cake in an upright position, and the other hand to squeeze the mixture out by applying pressure at the twisted end of the bag.

Press the bag to allow enough mixture to pipe onto the surface of the cake in the required design. Stop pressing the bag and lift sharply upwards to break the flow of the mixture. Repeat the process to pipe the design of your choice.

Illustrated below: rosettes, stars, shells and coil (piped with meringue star nozzles); leaf design (piped with parchment paper piping bag)

QUICK-MIX CAKE

250 ml (1 cup) self-raising flour	125 ml (¹/₂ cup) soft margarine
1 teaspoon baking powder	2 eggs
125 ml (¹/₂ cup) sugar	

Makes 2-egg quantity
Preparation time: 10 minutes
Cooking time: See individual recipes

1. Sift the flour and baking powder into a bowl. Add the sugar, margarine, eggs, and any flavourings (see below).
2. Mix together with a wooden spoon, then beat for 2–3 minutes until smooth and glossy; alternatively, beat with an electric mixer until just smooth. Use as required.

NOTE: This quantity is sufficient for 18 cup cakes; two 18 cm (7 inch) round cakes; an 18 cm (7 inch) square cake; a 20 cm (8 inch) round cake; a 23 cm (9 inch) ring cake.

Where a recipe specifies a 1-egg or 4-egg quantity, simply halve or double the above ingredients. For a 3-egg quantity, use half as much again, i.e. 375 ml (1½ cups) flour, 175 ml (¾ cup) sugar and margarine; 1½ teaspoons baking powder.

FLAVOURINGS

Chocolate. Add 1 tablespoon cocoa powder blended with 1 tablespoon boiling water.
Coffee. Add 2 teaspoons instant coffee blended with 1 teaspoon boiling water.
Citrus. Add 1 teaspoon grated orange, lemon or lime peel.

WHISKED SPONGE

2 eggs
50 ml (¹⁄4 cup) granulated
   sugar

125 ml (¹⁄2 cup)
   all-purpose flour
¹⁄2 teaspoon baking powder

1. Place the eggs and sugar in a heatproof bowl over a saucepan of hot water and whisk until thick and pale.
2. Remove the bowl from the heat and continue whisking until the whisk leaves a thick trail and the mixture is cool.
3. Sift the flour and baking powder onto the surface, add any flavourings (see below), and carefully fold in using a spatula or a large metal spoon. Use as required.

Makes 2-egg quantity
Preparation time: 10 minutes
Cooking time: See individual recipes

NOTE: This quantity is sufficient for 16–20 cup cakes; an 18 cm (7 inch) square cake; a 20 cm (8 inch) round cake; a 28 × 18 cm (11 × 7 inch) jelly roll pan.

Where a recipe specifies a 1-egg or 4-egg quantity, simply halve or double the above ingredients, but do not increase the baking powder. For a 3-egg quantity, use half as much again, i.e. 75 ml (⅓ cup) sugar and 175 ml (¾ cup) flour, but do not increase the baking powder.

FLAVOURINGS
Chocolate. Replace 2 tablespoons flour with cocoa.
Coffee. Add 2 teaspoons instant coffee powder to flour.
Citrus. Add 1 teaspoon grated orange, lemon or lime peel.
Nut. Replace 50 ml (¼ cup) flour with finely ground nuts.

GLACÉ ICING

500 ml (2 cups) icing sugar	*2–3 tablespoons boiling water*

Makes 1 quantity
Preparation time:
2 minutes
Freezing:
Not recommended

Sift the icing sugar into a bowl. Using a wooden spoon, gradually stir in the water until the icing is the consistency of thick cream. Use as required.

FLAVOURINGS
Chocolate. Sift 2 teaspoons cocoa with the icing sugar.
Fruit. Replace the water with any fruit juice.
Coffee. Replace the water with strong black coffee.

BUTTER ICING

125 ml (1/2 cup) butter, softened	*500 ml (2 cups) icing sugar, sifted* *1 teaspoon lemon juice*

Makes 1 quantity
Preparation time:
5 minutes
Freezing:
Recommended

1. Beat the butter in a bowl until light and fluffy.
2. Beat in the icing sugar a little at a time.
3. Beat in the lemon juice and any flavourings (see below). Use as required.

FLAVOURINGS
Chocolate. Add 1 tablespoon cocoa powder blended with 1 tablespoon boiling water.
Coffee. Add 2 teaspoons instant coffee blended with 1 teaspoon boiling water.
Citrus. Add 1 teaspoon finely grated lemon, orange or lime peel.

CHOCOLATE FUDGE ICING

125 g (4 oz) plain chocolate *50 ml (1/4 cup) butter*	*1 egg, beaten* *375 ml (11/2 cups) icing sugar, sifted*

Makes 1 quantity
Preparation time:
5 minutes
Freezing:
Recommended

1. Place the chocolate and butter in a heatproof bowl over a pan of hot water until melted, stirring occasionally.
2. Remove the bowl from the heat and beat in the egg. Stir in the icing sugar, then beat until smooth.
3. Pour immediately over a cake for a smooth finish or leave to cool for a thicker spreading consistency.

QUICK FROSTING

A quickly-made frosting for coating large or small cakes.

50 ml (¼ cup) butter
3 tablespoons milk

500 ml (2 cups) icing
sugar, sifted

1. Place the ingredients in a heatproof bowl over a saucepan of hot water.
2. Stir occasionally until melted, then beat with a wooden spoon until smooth. Use immediately as required.

Makes 1 quantity
Preparation time:
5 minutes
Freezing:
Recommended

FLAVOURINGS
Caramel. Replace 50 ml (¼ cup) of the icing sugar with dark brown sugar.
Fruit. Replace the milk with any fruit juice.
Coffee. Replace the milk with strong black coffee.
Chocolate. Sift 1 tablespoon cocoa with the icing sugar.

CRÈME AU BEURRE

A light-textured butter cream for gâteaux and small cakes.

75 ml (⅓ cup) sugar
4 tablespoons water
2 egg yolks, beaten

150 ml (⅔ cup) unsalted
butter, softened

1. Place the sugar and water in a saucepan and heat very gently until the sugar has dissolved, stirring occasionally.
2. Boil rapidly for about 1 minute, without stirring, until the syrup reaches 'thread stage': to test, place a little syrup between 2 teaspoons, then pull apart—a thread of syrup should form.
3. Pour the syrup in a steady stream onto the egg yolks, whisking all the time. Continue whisking until the mixture is thick and pale.
4. Beat the butter until light and fluffy, then gradually add the egg mixture, beating well after each addition, until thick and fluffy.
5. Add any flavourings (see below) and use immediately.

Makes 1 quantity
Preparation time:
10 minutes
Freezing:
Not recommended

FLAVOURINGS
Chocolate. Add 25 g (1 oz) melted chocolate.
Coffee. Add 2 teaspoons instant coffee powder with the syrup.
Citrus. Add 1 teaspoon grated orange, lemon or lime peel.

LEMON RINGS

1-egg quantity lemon
   Quick-Mix Cake mixture
   (page 14)

1 quantity lemon
   Quick Frosting (page
   17)
peel of 1 lemon and 1 lime

Makes 8
Preparation time:
25 minutes
Cooking time:
15 minutes
Freezing:
Recommended

1. Divide the cake mixture between 8 small greased ring moulds, placed on a baking sheet. Bake in a preheated oven, 170°C/325°F, for 15 minutes, until well risen and springy to touch. Invert onto a wire rack, well apart. Leave to cool.
2. Place the wire rack over a plate. Quickly spoon the frosting over each sponge ring to coat evenly; allow the excess frosting to fall onto the plate and re-use if necessary. Leave to set.
3. Using a small petal cutter, cut out petal shapes from the lemon and lime peel and use to decorate the lemon rings.

MINSTREL BOXES

2-egg quantity Whisked
   Sponge mixture
   (page 15)
175 g (6 oz) each plain
   and white chocolate,
   melted separately
4 tablespoons redcurrant
   jelly, warmed

150 ml (⅔ cup) natural
   yogurt
150 ml (⅔ cup) whipping
   cream, whipped
TO DECORATE:
250 g (8 oz) raspberries
16 sugar-frosted flowers
   (see page 10)

Makes 16
Preparation time:
35 minutes
Cooking time:
20–25 minutes
Freezing:
Recommended,
without decoration

1. Grease and line an 18 cm (7 inch) square cake pan.
2. Place the sponge mixture in the pan and bake in a preheated oven, 180°C/350°F, for 20–25 minutes, until risen and springy to touch. Cool on a wire rack.
3. Cut out two 30 × 20 cm (12 × 8 inch) rectangles of foil. Cover one with the plain chocolate and the other with the white, spreading thinly and evenly. Leave for about 10 minutes, until just set.
4. Using a sharp knife and ruler, cut each chocolate rectangle into about forty 3.5 cm (1½ inch) squares (this allows for any breakages).
5. Cut the cake into sixteen 3.5 cm (1½ inch) squares and brush the sides with redcurrant jelly. Press on alternate plain and white chocolate squares to make boxes.
6. Fold the yogurt into the cream and spoon into each box. Decorate with raspberries and frosted flowers.

HARLEQUIN SLICES

2-egg quantity Quick-Mix
    Cake mixture (page 14)
1 quantity Butter Icing
    (page 16)

few drops pink and green
    food colourings

1. Grease and line a 20 cm (8 inch) square cake pan.
2. Place the cake mixture in the prepared pan and bake in a preheated oven, 170°C/325°F, for 30–35 minutes, until well risen and springy to touch. Turn out and cool on a wire rack.
3. Colour one third of the butter icing pale green and one third pale pink with the food colourings.
4. Place the 3 different icings in separate parchment paper piping bags and snip off the ends (see page 12).
5. Pipe alternate coloured lines over the top of the cake. Leave in a cool place to set.
6. Cut the cake into 5 thin strips, then cut each strip diagonally into 4 diamond shapes.

Makes 20
Preparation time:
30 minutes
Cooking time:
30–35 minutes
Freezing:
Recommended

CHOCOLATE FRUIT CUPS

Fill these chocolate cups with fruits in season.

*175 g (6 oz) plain or milk
  chocolate, melted
25 g (1 oz) ratafia biscuits,
  crushed
175 g (6 oz) cherries,
  pitted*

*1 kiwi fruit, peeled and
  sliced
250 g (8 oz) carton light
  cream cheese
4 tablespoons sour cream
2 teaspoons granulated
  sugar*

Makes 10
Preparation time:
15 minutes, plus
setting time
Freezing:
Not recommended

1. Place 10 paper cake cases in a muffin pan. Place a teaspoonful of chocolate in each case and brush the chocolate over the base and up the side to coat evenly. Chill for about 15 minutes to set hard.

2. Carefully peel off the paper cases and arrange the chocolate cups on a serving plate.

3. Sprinkle the ratafias over the base of each case.

4. Set aside 10 cherries and 5 kiwi fruit slices. Chop the remaining fruit and place in the cases.

5. Beat together the cheese, cream and sugar until smooth. Place in a nylon piping bag fitted with a medium meringue star nozzle and pipe a swirl into each chocolate case. Top each with a cherry and a halved kiwi slice.

MADELEINES

3 eggs, separated
4 tablespoons sugar
1 teaspoon rosewater
125 ml (½ cup)
*   all-purpose flour, sifted*

25 g (1 oz) plain
*   chocolate, melted*
icing sugar to dredge

1. Place the egg yolks, sugar and rosewater in a bowl and whisk until pale and foamy.
2. Whisk the egg whites until stiff, then fold half into the egg mixture, using a spatula, until smooth.
3. Add the flour and remaining egg white, folding in carefully. Place in a nylon piping bag fitted with a 1 cm (½ inch) plain nozzle and pipe into a well greased and lightly floured madeleine tray, filling each mould to the top.
4. Bake in a preheated oven, 180°C/350°F, for 10–15 minutes, until pale in colour but firm to touch. Cool on a wire rack. Re-grease the moulds and repeat with the remaining mixture.
5. Using a glazing brush, diagonally coat half of each madeleine with chocolate. Leave to set on the wire rack.
6. Cover the chocolate-covered cake with paper towels and dredge the plain half with icing sugar.

Makes about 28
Preparation time:
15 minutes
Cooking time:
10–15 minutes
Freezing:
Recommended

PASTEL FONDANTS

If the ready-made melting fondant is unobtainable use ready-to-roll fondant icing, colouring it before use.

*2-egg quantity Whisked
    Sponge mixture (page
    15)*
*4 tablespoons Apricot
    Glaze (page 46)*
*1 kg (2 lb) ready-made
    melting fondant*

25 g (1 oz) Marzipan
5 whole blanched almonds
*few drops pink, yellow and
    green food colourings*
*5 piped chocolate pieces
    (page 9)*
5 piped flowers (page 51)

Makes 20
Preparation time:
45 minutes, plus
setting time
Cooking time:
20–25 minutes
Freezing:
Recommended at
end of stage 3

1. Grease and line a 20 cm (8 inch) square cake pan.
2. Place the sponge mixture in the prepared pan and bake in a preheated oven, 180°C/350°F, for 20–25 minutes, until well risen and springy to touch. Turn out and cool on a wire rack.
3. Cut the cake into 5 rounds using a 3.5 cm (1½ inch) plain cutter, and 5 oval shapes using a 5 cm (2 inch) cutter. Cut the remaining cake into five 3.5 cm (1½ inch) squares and 5 triangles.
4. Brush all shapes with apricot glaze and leave overnight.
5. Place the fondant in a heatproof bowl over a pan of simmering water until melted, stirring occasionally.
6. Shape half of the marzipan into 5 squares and place on the square cakes. Shape 5 little balls of marzipan, press an almond into each, then place in the centre of the triangles. Place on the wire rack over a plate.
7. Keep the fondant over the hot water and dilute with a little hot water if it is too thick to thinly coat the back of the spoon. Pour 1 tablespoon over each triangle to coat evenly, allowing the excess icing to fall onto the plate. Remove each cake as it sets and trim off icing at the base.
8. Return the excess fondant to the bowl and heat gently until melted. Colour it very pale pink with food colouring and use a third to cover the square cakes, as described above. Colour the remaining pink fondant pale yellow and use half to cover the oval cakes. Colour the remaining yellow fondant green and use to cover the round cakes.
9. Fill a parchment paper piping bag with green fondant and snip off the end (see page 12). Pipe a spiral thread of icing over each green round cake, then pipe a zig-zag over the white triangles.
10. Place a piped chocolate piece on each oval cake and attach a sugar flower to each square cake with icing.
11. Place all the cakes in paper cake cases to serve.

ORANGE BOATS

A pretty way to turn a sponge mixture into small cakes
using crème au beurre, oranges and nuts.

*1-egg quantity orange
  Whisked Sponge mixture
  (page 15)
1 quantity orange Crème
  au Beurre (page 17)*

*40 g (1½ oz) walnuts,
  chopped finely
3 oranges, peeled and
  segmented (all pith
  removed)*

1. Divide the sponge mixture between 12 greased boat moulds on a baking sheet and bake in a preheated oven, 180°C/350°F, for 10 minutes, until well risen and springy to touch. Turn onto a wire rack to cool.
2. Cover the base of each sponge boat with crème au beurre and coat evenly with the walnuts.
3. Place the remaining crème au beurre in a nylon piping bag fitted with a small star meringue nozzle and pipe shells on each sponge boat. Decorate with the oranges.

Makes 12
Preparation time:
25 minutes
Cooking time:
10 minutes
Freezing:
Recommended,
without orange
segments

COFFEE-FROSTED RING

*2-egg quantity coffee
  Quick-Mix Cake mixture
  (page 14)*

*1 quantity caramel
  Quick Frosting (page
  17)*

*sugar-frosted rose petals
  (see page 10)*

**Makes one 23 cm
(9 inch) ring cake
Preparation time:**
20 minutes
Cooking time:
30–35 minutes
Freezing:
Recommended,
without frosted
petals

1. Turn the cake mixture into a greased 23 cm (9 inch) ring pan and bake in a preheated oven, 170°C/325°F, for 30–35 minutes, until well risen and springy to touch. Turn out and cool on a wire rack.
2. Place over a plate and pour over the frosting all at once to coat evenly. Leave until almost set.
3. Place the cake on a plate and arrange the frosted petals on the cake.

CHOCOLATE FUDGE CAKE

The icing can be used for piping if left to thicken. Icing sugar patterns make a good contrast.

*3-egg quantity chocolate
  Quick-Mix Cake mixture
  (page 14)*
3 tablespoons cherry jam

*1 quantity Chocolate Fudge
  Icing (page 16)*
2 tablespoons icing sugar

**Makes one 20 cm
(8 inch) square
cake
Preparation time:**
25 minutes
Cooking time:
30–35 minutes
Freezing:
Recommended

1. Grease and line a 20 cm (8 inch) square cake pan.
2. Turn the cake mixture into the prepared pan and bake in a preheated oven, 170°C/325°F, for 30–35 minutes, until well risen and firm to touch. Turn out and cool on a wire rack.
3. Split the cake in half and sandwich together with the jam. Place on the wire rack over a plate.
4. Pour the chocolate fudge icing all over the cake and smooth with a palette knife to cover evenly. Tap the rack to allow the excess icing to fall onto the plate. Transfer the cake to a flat plate or cake board.
5. Place the remaining icing in a nylon piping bag fitted with a small star meringue nozzle.
6. Cut out 10 strips of paper 23 × 1 cm (9 × ½ inch) and arrange over the top of the cake in a lattice design.
7. Sift the icing sugar over the top of the cake. Carefully remove the paper strips.
8. Pipe a shell edging around the base of the cake and leave for about 15 minutes, to set.

RASPBERRY JELLY ROLL

*3-egg quantity Whisked
    Sponge mixture (page
    15)
250 g (8 oz) raspberries*

*150 ml (²/₃ cup) whipping
    cream, whipped
1 quantity Glacé Icing
    (page 16)
pink food colouring*

**Makes one jelly
roll**
Preparation time:
20 minutes
Cooking time:
10–15 minutes
Freezing:
Recommended at
end of stage 5

1. Grease and line a 33 × 23 cm (13 × 9 inch) jelly roll pan.
2. Turn the sponge mixture into the prepared pan and bake in a preheated oven, 180°C/350°F, for 10–15 minutes, until well risen and springy to touch.
3. Turn onto sugared non-stick parchment paper, peel off the lining paper and trim off the edges. Roll up from a shorter side, enclosing the sugared paper, and leave to cool.
4. Set aside 6 raspberries for decoration. Fold the rest into the whipped cream.
5. Carefully unroll the jelly roll and remove the paper. Spread the raspberry cream mixture evenly over the surface, re-roll and place on a wire rack.
6. Colour the glacé icing pale pink with food colouring. Pour over the roll to cover completely and leave until set. Place the reserved raspberries in a row on top of the jelly roll to serve.

VANILLA CAKE

This cake can be decorated with any bought decorations, but the sugar flowers used here are quite effective.

2-egg quantity Quick-Mix
   Cake mixture (page 14)
1 quantity Butter
   Icing (page 16)

25 g (1 oz) crunch-nut
   topping
15 g (1/2 oz) angelica
13–15 sugar flowers

Makes one 18 cm (7 inch) round cake
Preparation time: 25 minutes
Cooking time: 20–25 minutes
Freezing: Recommended

1. Grease and line the bottom of two 18 cm (7 inch) round cake pans.
2. Divide the cake mixture between the prepared pans and bake in a preheated oven, 170°C/325°F, for 20–25 minutes, until well risen and firm to touch. Turn out and cool on a wire rack.
3. Sandwich the cakes together with a third of the butter icing.
4. Half-fill a parchment paper piping bag with butter icing and snip the point for a leaf design (see page 12).
5. Spread the remaining icing evenly over the top and side of the cake. Coat the side with crunch-nut topping.
6. Cut the angelica into 5 mm (1/4 inch) wide strips, then cut into diamond shapes.
7. Pipe a leaf border around the top edge of the cake and pipe a leaf circle in the centre. Arrange the angelica leaves and sugar flowers on top of the cake.

LEMON AND CHOCOLATE BATTENBURG

Various flavoured cakes can be used for a battenburg—try coffee and orange, for a change. Use either homemade marzipan or the white marzipan you can buy ready made.

2-egg quantity Quick-Mix Cake mixture (page 14)
1 tablespoon cocoa powder blended with 1 tablespoon boiling water
1/2 teaspoon grated lemon peel

few drops yellow food colouring
3 tablespoons Apricot Glaze (page 46)
350 g (12 oz) Marzipan (page 45)
1/2 tablespoon cocoa powder

Makes one battenburg
Preparation time: 20 minutes
Cooking time: 40–45 minutes
Freezing: Recommended

1. Grease and line an 18 cm (7 inch) square cake pan and place a double strip of parchment paper along the centre to divide the pan in half.
2. Divide the cake mixture in half. Add the blended cocoa to one half, and the lemon peel and yellow food colouring to the other half.
3. Place the lemon mixture on one side of the dividing paper in the pan and the chocolate mixture on the other. Bake in a preheated oven, 170°C/325°F, for 40–45 minutes, until well risen and springy to touch.
4. Turn out carefully onto a wire rack and separate to cool, removing all the parchment paper.
5. Trim the edges of the cakes carefully to neaten, then cut in half lengthways, making 4 strips. Sandwich the strips together with apricot glaze, alternating the colours, to make a square.
6. Colour the marzipan yellow with food colouring, then roll out to an oblong, the same length as the cake and 4 times the width, trimming as necessary.
7. Brush the cake with apricot glaze and place it across one short side of the marzipan. Turn the cake 3 times, to enclose completely in the marzipan, then trim the edges to neaten, sealing the join underneath.
8. Knead the cocoa powder into two thirds of the marzipan trimmings until smooth and evenly coloured, then divide in half. Roll each piece into a 23 cm (9 inch) strip. Roll out the remaining yellow marzipan to a similar-length strip.
9. Plait the 3 pieces together and arrange on top of the battenburg, trimming to fit. Attach with a little glaze.

CITRUS SPONGE CAKE

3-egg quantity lemon
  Quick-Mix Cake mixture
  (page 14)
2 tablespoons lemon curd

1 quantity orange Crème
  au Beurre (page 17)
peel of 1 lime and
  1 orange

1. Grease and line the bottom of two 20 cm (8 inch) round cake pans.

2. Divide the cake mixture between the prepared pans and bake in a preheated oven, 170°C/325°F, for 25–30 minutes, until well risen and firm to touch. Turn out and cool on a wire rack.

3. Sandwich the cakes together with the lemon curd.

4. Cover the side and top of the cake with the icing. Smooth evenly then mark a pattern with a palette knife.

5. Using a small petal cutter, if you have one, or a small sharp knife, cut out petal shapes from the lime and orange peel and use to decorate the top edge of the cake.

6. Make a flower design in the centre using petal shapes and strips of peel.

Makes one 20 cm (8 inch) round cake
Preparation time: 25 minutes
Cooking time: 25–30 minutes
Freezing: Recommended

LIME CHEESE GÂTEAU

An 'instant' gâteau, made with trifle sponges, soft cheese and limes—light and refreshing. If you have time, use a 3-egg quantity whisked sponge (see page 15), cooked in a 33 × 23 cm (13 × 9 inch) jelly roll pan, in place of the trifle sponges. (See page 26 for baking instructions.)

250 ml (8 oz) carton light
  cream cheese
125 ml (½ cup) sugar
3 eggs, separated
grated peel and juice of
  2 limes
12 trifle sponges

TO DECORATE:
150 ml (⅔ cup) whipping
  cream
1½ tablespoons natural
  yogurt
75 g (3 oz) pistachio nuts,
  skinned
1 lime, cut into thin
  wedges

Makes one 20 cm (8 inch) gâteau
Preparation time: 25 minutes, plus chilling
Freezing: Recommended

1. Place the cheese and sugar in a bowl and beat with a wooden spoon until smooth.
2. Beat in the egg yolks until well blended, then stir in the lime peel and juice; the mixture may appear curdled.
3. Whisk the egg whites until stiff, then fold into the lime mixture.
4. Line the base and side of a 20 cm (8 inch) round cake pan with plastic wrap or foil.
5. Cut each sponge cake horizontally into 3 layers and use to line the base and side of the pan. Pour in half of the lime mixture. Cover with a layer of sponge pieces and pour in the remaining lime mixture. Top with the remaining sponge pieces. Cover with plastic wrap or foil and chill overnight.
6. Whip the cream and yogurt together until thick. Place 3 tablespoons in a nylon piping bag fitted with a medium star meringue nozzle and set aside.
7. Set aside about 12 pistachios for decoration; chop the remainder. Cover the top and side of the gâteau with cream, then coat the side with the chopped nuts.
8. Pipe the reserved cream in swirls around the top edge of the gâteau and top with the reserved nuts. Arrange the lime wedges in the centre.

PRALINE COFFEE GÂTEAU

4-egg quantity Whisked Sponge mixture (page 15, replacing 50 ml (¹/₄ cup) of the flour with ground almonds 125 ml (¹/₂ cup) sugar	*4 tablespoons water 75 g (3 oz) whole blanched almonds 300 ml (1¹/₄ cups) whipping cream 2 teaspoons strong coffee*

Makes one 20 cm (8 inch) gâteau
Preparation time: 30–40 minutes
Cooking time: 20–25 minutes
Freezing: Recommended at end of stage 2

1. Grease and line the bottom of two 20 cm (8 inch) round cake pans.
2. Divide the sponge mixture between the prepared pans and bake in a preheated oven, 180°C/350°F, for 20–25 minutes, until well risen and springy to touch. Turn out and cool on a wire rack.
3. Cover 2 baking sheets with foil and brush with oil.
4. Place the sugar and water in a pan and heat gently, stirring occasionally, until melted. Add the almonds and bring to the boil, without stirring; boil rapidly until the mixture begins to turn golden brown. Remove from the heat and allow the bubbles to subside.
5. Using a spoon dipped in oil, lift out 10 separate almonds and place well apart at one end of one foil-lined baking sheet. Drizzle a thread of the caramel in an abstract pattern onto the other end of the baking sheet to cover an area about 3.5 cm (1½ inches) square. Repeat to make 10 designs. Leave to set.
6. Pour the remaining caramel and nuts onto the other baking sheet. Leave to set.
7. Place the cream and coffee in a bowl and whip until thick. Divide the coffee cream in half.
8. Crush the caramel and nut mixture with a rolling pin or place in a food processor to chop finely into praline. Add half of the crushed praline to one portion of the coffee cream.
9. Split each cake in half horizontally and sandwich the layers together with two thirds of the praline cream.
10. Cover the side of the cake with the remaining praline cream and coat evenly with the remaining praline. Place on a serving plate.
11. Cover the top with half of the remaining coffee cream and mark a pattern with a palette knife. Put the remaining coffee cream in a nylon piping bag fitted with a small star meringue nozzle and pipe the reserved coffee cream in swirls around the top edge of the gâteau.
12. Just before serving, carefully position the caramel pieces and nuts around the edge of the gâteau.

CHOCOLATE LEAF GÂTEAU

150 ml (²/₃ cup) sugar
300 ml (1¼ cups)
   self-raising flour, sifted
50 ml (¼ cup) cocoa
   powder
3 tablespoons oil
2–3 tablespoons boiling
   water
5 eggs, separated

TO DECORATE:
300 g (10 oz) plain
   chocolate
300 ml (1¼ cups)
   whipping cream
9 sugar-frosted flowers (see
   page 10)

Makes one 20 cm (8 inch) square gâteau
Preparation time: 30 minutes
Cooking time: 35–40 minutes
Freezing: Recommended, without sugar flowers

1. Grease and line a 20 cm (8 inch) square cake pan.
2. Place the sugar, flour, cocoa, oil, water and egg yolks in a bowl. Mix together with a wooden spoon, then beat until smooth.
3. Whisk the egg whites until stiff, then fold into the mixture using a large metal spoon.
4. Pour the mixture into the prepared pan and bake in a preheated oven, 180°C/350°F, for 35–40 minutes, until well risen and firm to touch. Turn out carefully and cool on a wire rack.
5. Melt 125 g (4 oz) of the chocolate in a heatproof bowl over a pan of hot water; use to make 27 chocolate rose leaves (see page 9).
6. Whip half of the cream until thick, then whisk into the remaining cooled melted chocolate.
7. Cover the top and sides of the cake evenly with the chocolate cream, reserving 2–3 tablespoons for piping. Chill the cake for 10 minutes.
8. Place the remaining chocolate and cream in a pan and heat gently, stirring occasionally, until the chocolate has melted. Leave until cool and thick enough to coat the back of a spoon.
9. Place the cake on the wire rack over a plate and pour the chocolate icing all over to cover evenly. When the icing has stopped falling off the cake, place the cake on a serving plate.
10. Mix the chocolate from the plate with the reserved chocolate cream and stir together until thick. Place in a nylon piping bag fitted with a small star meringue nozzle and pipe a shell border around the base of the cake. Place a sugar-frosted flower at each corner of the cake. Decorate the top with the remaining frosted flowers and the chocolate leaves.

HAZELNUT STRAWBERRY GÂTEAU

A moist hazelnut cake sandwiched between crisp meringue layers and a strawberry-cream filling. This gâteau is equally delicious made with fresh cherries during their short season. Simply halve and pit the cherries.

FOR THE CAKE:
50 ml (1/4 cup) soft margarine
50 ml (1/4 cup) sugar
50 g (2 oz) hazelnuts, roasted and ground
2 tablespoons corn starch
1 egg
FOR THE MERINGUE:
125 ml (1/2 cup) fine sugar

75 g (3 oz) hazelnuts, roasted and ground
2 egg whites
FOR THE FILLING:
150 ml (2/3 cup) whipping cream
3 tablespoons natural yogurt
350 g (12 oz) strawberries, sliced

Makes one 18 cm (7 inch) gâteau
Preparation time: 30 minutes
Cooking time: 20–25 minutes
Freezing: Recommended, without strawberry decoration

1. Grease and line a shallow 18 cm (7 inch) square cake pan.
2. Place all the cake ingredients in a bowl and beat with a wooden spoon until smooth. Place in the prepared pan and level the top. Set aside while making the meringue.
3. Line 2 baking sheets with non-stick parchment paper and draw an 18 cm (7 inch) square on each.
4. Place half of the sugar and the hazelnuts in a bowl and mix together well. Whisk the egg whites until stiff, then whisk in the remaining sugar. Carefully fold in the hazelnut and sugar mixture.
5. Fill a nylon piping bag, fitted with a 1 cm (1/2 inch) plain meringue nozzle, with half the mixture and pipe a lattice design within one marked square, then a row of peaks around the outside to join the lattice.
6. Spread the remaining mixture within the other marked square to cover evenly.
7. Bake the cake and meringue squares in a preheated oven, 170°C/325°F, for 20–25 minutes, until the cake is pale in colour and springy to touch, and the meringue is lightly browned and crisp. Turn out the cake and cool on a wire rack. Leave the meringue on the paper until cool, then peel off the paper carefully.
8. Whip the cream and yogurt together and fold in two thirds of the strawberries. Cover the plain meringue square with half of the mixture. Place the cake on top.
9. Spread the remaining strawberry mixture over the cake and top with the lattice meringue. Fill the lattice with the reserved strawberries. Chill until required.

APPLE AND MARRON GÂTEAU

3 eggs
125 ml (½ cup) sugar
1 teaspoon vanilla extract
175 ml (¾ cup)
  self-raising flour
398 ml (14 oz) can
  unsweetened chestnut
  purée
300 ml (1¼ cups)
  whipping cream

2 teaspoons liquid honey
2 green-skinned eating
  apples, cored
1 tablespoon lemon juice
2 oranges
50 g (2 oz) walnuts,
  chopped finely
2 tablespoons Apricot
  Glaze (page 46)

**Makes one 23 cm
(9 inch) gâteau
Preparation time:**
30–40 minutes
Cooking time:
10–15 minutes
Freezing:
Recommended at
end of stage 6

1. Line 3 baking sheets with non-stick parchment paper and mark a 23 cm (9 inch) circle on each.
2. Whisk together the eggs, sugar and vanilla extract until thick and pale.
3. Sift the flour over the surface of the mixture and fold in using a large metal spoon or spatula.
4. Divide the mixture between the circles and spread evenly to the edges.
5. Bake in a preheated oven, 200°C/400°F, for 10–15 minutes, until lightly coloured and springy to touch.
6. Cool on the paper until firm, then peel off the paper and cool on a wire rack.
7. Place the chestnut purée, half of the cream and the honey in a bowl and beat until smooth. Place 2 tablespoons in a nylon piping bag fitted with a small star meringue nozzle and set aside for decoration.
8. Whip the remaining cream until thick.
9. Cut the apples into thin slices and toss in the lemon juice, then strain. Chop one third of the slices finely.
10. Finely grate the orange peel. Cut the orange flesh into segments, discarding all pith.
11. Place one cake on a flat serving plate or cake board and spread with a quarter of the chestnut mixture. Sprinkle with half of the orange peel and chopped apple, and top with a third of the cream. Repeat the layers, finishing with a layer of chestnut mixture.
12. Top with the remaining cake. Cover the side and top with the last quarter of the chestnut mixture, then coat the side evenly with the walnuts.
13. Arrange the apple slices on the gâteau, with a circle of orange segments in the centre. Brush with the glaze.
14. Pipe the reserved chestnut mixture as stars around the top edge and in the centre. Use the remaining cream to pipe on top of the chestnut stars. Chill until required.

ELABORATE CAKE DECORATING

EQUIPMENT

In addition to the basic equipment given on pages 6–7, you will need the following items.

Straight edge. A special icing ruler used to obtain flat smooth icing on top of a cake.

Side scraper. For smoothing the side(s) of a cake.

Muslin. Ideal for covering a bowl of royal icing to prevent a skin forming; being white it will not impart any colour.

Brushes. Buy fine artists' brushes for painting piped flowers and other decorations with food colouring; for coating flowers and leaves with egg white before frosting; also useful when making run-outs.

Flower nails. Useful when piping flowers. Available from kitchen shops. Or make your own using a cork and nail.

Small cutters. Used for cutting out marzipan, moulding icing and sugar paste shapes, such as numbers, letters, petals, leaves and flowers.

Tweezers. Indispensable for delicate work. Buy a pair with rounded ends.

Stamens. These are available in different colours from specialist equipment suppliers, to thread through the centre of sugar flowers (illustrated opposite).

Dowel. Different sizes of wooden dowel are useful to place leaves and petals on to dry—to give them a good shape. Wooden spoon handles are good alternatives.

PREPARING A CAKE PAN FOR FRUIT CAKES

Use a good-quality fixed-base deep cake pan. Make sure you use the exact size stated in the recipe, otherwise the depth and cooking time of the cake will be affected. Measure the pan across the base, not the top. Cake pans are available in standard sizes, 15–23 cm (6–10 inches), from kitchen shops. Other sizes and shaped pans are obtainable from specialist cake decorating shops.

1. Place the cake pan on double thickness waxed paper or non-stick parchment paper and draw around the base. Cut out the marked shape.

2. Cut a strip of double thickness waxed paper or non-stick parchment paper long enough to wrap around the outside of the pan with a small overlap and wide enough to stand 2.5 cm (1 inch) above the top of the pan.

3. Brush the base and side(s) of the pan with melted shortening or oil. Place the cut-out paper base shape in the pan and smooth out the creases.

4. Place the double strip of paper inside the pan, pressing well against the side(s) and making sharp creases where it fits into corners.

5. Brush the base and side papers with melted fat or oil.

6. Place a double thickness strip of brown paper around the outside of the pan and tie securely with string. This prevents the outside of the cake being overcooked.

7. Line a baking sheet with 3 or 4 layers of brown paper and place the pan on top. This prevents the base of the cake being overcooked.

RICH FRUIT CAKE

This recipe makes a super rich moist fruit cake, suitable for any special occasion. It also allows the cake to be made in stages, particularly useful if you are making more than one cake. The quantities have been worked out so that each cake size is the same depth. This is particularly important if you are making a tiered wedding cake, when each cake must be the same height.

All the fruit can be prepared and soaked overnight in brandy, whisky or sherry and the cake made the next day if time is short. If more than one cake is being made, and the cooking time cannot be fitted in on the same day, place the mixture in the pans, cover with plastic wrap and leave in a cool place overnight.

Wrap the cooked, cooled cakes in a double layer of foil and store in a cool place. *Never* seal in an airtight container as this may encourage mould growth.

Rich fruit cakes keep well. Although they can be eaten when first made, these cakes mature with keeping, but they are best eaten within 3 months. If you are going to keep a fruit cake for several months, add the alcohol a little at a time at monthly intervals.

Square Cake Round Cake	□ 13 cm (5 inch) O 15 cm (6 inch)	□ 15 cm (6 inch) O 18 cm (7 inch)	□ 18 cm (7 inch) O 20 cm (8 inch)
Raisins	150 g (5 oz)	200 g (7 oz)	275 g (9 oz)
Sultana raisins	150 g (5 oz)	200 g (7 oz)	275 g (9 oz)
Currants	125 g (4 oz)	150 g (5 oz)	200 g (7 oz)
Glacé cherries, halved	75 g (3 oz)	75 g (3 oz)	150 g (5 oz)
Cut mixed peel	25 g (1 oz)	40 g (1½ oz)	50 g (2 oz)
Sliced almonds	25 g (1 oz)	40 g (1½ oz)	50 g (2 oz)
Orange peel, coarsely grated	1 teaspoon	1½ teaspoons	2 teaspoons
Orange juice	1 tablespoon	2 tablespoons	3 tablespoons
Brandy, whisky or sherry	1 tablespoon	2 tablespoons	3 tablespoons
All-purpose flour	375 ml (1½ cups)	425 ml (1¾ cups)	550 ml (2¼ cups)
Ground allspice	1 teaspoon	2 teaspoons	2½ teaspoons
Ground almonds	25 g (1 oz)	40 g (1½ oz)	50 g (2 oz)
Dark brown sugar	175 ml (¾ cup)	250 ml (1 cup)	325 ml (1⅓ cups)
Butter or margarine, softened	125 ml (½ cup)	150 ml (⅔ cup)	250 ml (1 cup)
Molasses	½ tablespoon	1 tablespoon	1½ tablespoons
Eggs	2	3	4
Cooking times	2¼ hours	2¼ hours	2½ hours

1. Mix the raisins, sultana raisins, currants, glacé cherries, peel, sliced almonds, orange peel and juice, and brandy, whisky or sherry in a large mixing bowl.

2. Sift the flour and spice into another bowl, add the ground almonds, sugar, butter or margarine, molasses and eggs, mix well, then beat for 2–3 minutes until smooth and glossy. Fold in to the fruit mixture until evenly blended.

3. Spoon the mixture into the prepared pan (see page 41) and spread evenly over the base and into the corners. Give the pan a few sharp bangs to level the mixture and remove any air pockets. Smooth the surface with the back of a metal spoon dipped in hot water, making a slight depression in the centre.

4. Bake in a preheated oven, 140°C/275°F, following the chart cooking time guide. Test the cake to see if it is cooked 15 minutes before the suggested time. If cooked, a skewer inserted into the centre of the cake will come out clean. If the cake is not cooked, re-test at 15 minute intervals.

5. Leave the cake in the pan until cold.

6. Turn the cake out of the pan but do not remove the lining paper. Use half the quantity of brandy, whisky or sherry to spoon over the top of the cake.

7. Wrap the cake in double foil and store in a cool dry place for a week. Spoon over remaining brandy, whisky or sherry, re-wrap and store upside down.

Square Cake Round Cake	□ 20 cm (8 inch) ○ 23 cm (9 inch)	□ 23 cm (9 inch) ○ 25 cm (10 inch)	□ 25 cm (10 inch) ○ 28 cm (11 inch)
Raisins	325 g (11 oz)	400 g (14 oz)	550 g (1 lb 2 oz)
Sultana raisins	325 g (11 oz)	400 g (14 oz)	550 g (1 lb 2 oz)
Currants	275 g (9 oz)	350 g (12 oz)	425 g (15 oz)
Glacé cherries halved	175 g (6 oz)	200 g (7 oz)	250 g (8 oz)
Cut mixed peel	75 g (3 oz)	125 g (4 oz)	175 g (6 oz)
Sliced almonds	75 g (3 oz)	125 g (4 oz)	175 g (6 oz)
Orange peel, coarsely grated	2½ teaspoons	1 tablespoon	1½ tablespoons
Orange juice	4 tablespoons	5 tablespoons	6 tablespoons
Brandy, whisky or sherry	4 tablespoons	5 tablespoons	6 tablespoons
All-purpose flour	650 ml (2⅔ cups)	850 ml (3½ cups)	1150 ml (4⅔ cups)
Ground allspice	1 tablespoon	1½ tablespoons	2 tablespoons
Ground almonds	65 g (2½ oz)	75 g (3 oz)	100 g (3½ oz)
Dark brown sugar	425 ml (1¾ cups)	625 ml (2½ cups)	800 ml (3¼ cups)
Butter or margarine, softened	300 ml (1¼ cups)	375 ml (1½ cups)	500 ml (2 cups)
Molasses	2 tablespoons	2½ tablespoons	3 tablespoons
Eggs	5	7	8
Cooking times	3¼ hours	3¼ hours	3½ hours

LIGHT FRUIT CAKE

This recipe makes a light, moist farmhouse-type fruit cake. It can be made instead of the rich fruit cake for any of the celebration cakes (on pages 60–79), if you prefer. It will keep for up to 4 weeks and can be marzipanned, iced and decorated quite successfully.

1. Prepare the cake pan (see page 41).
2. Place the mixed fruit, glacé cherries, lemon peel and sherry in a large mixing bowl and stir well.
3. Sift the flour and mixed spice into another bowl. Add the sugar, butter or margarine and eggs. Mix together with a wooden spoon until smooth and glossy; alternatively, beat for 1–2 minutes using an electric mixer.
4. Add to the fruit mixture and stir gently until well mixed.
5. Spoon the mixture into the prepared cake pan and spread evenly over the base and into the corners. Give the pan a few sharp bangs to level the mixture and remove any air pockets. Smooth the surface with the back of a metal spoon, making a fairly deep depression in the centre.
6. Bake in a preheated oven, 150°C/300°F, following the chart cooking time guide. Test the cake 15 minutes before the end of the given cooking time. If cooked, a skewer inserted into the centre of the cake will come out clean. If the cake is not cooked, re-test at 15 minute intervals.
7. Leave to cool in the pan.
8. Wrap in foil and store in a cool place for up to 4 weeks.

Square cake Round cake	☐ 18 cm (7 inch) ○ 20 cm (8 inch)	☐ 20 cm (8 inch) ○ 23 cm (9 inch)	☐ 23 cm (9 inch) ○ 25 cm (10 inch)
Mixed dried fruit	400 g (14 oz)	650 g (1 lb 5 oz)	875 g (1¾ lb)
Glacé cherries, halved	75 g (3 oz)	125 g (4 oz)	175 g (6 oz)
Lemon peel, coarsely grated	2 teaspoons	2½ teaspoons	1 tablespoon
Sherry	1 tablespoon	1½ tablespoons	2 tablespoons
All-purpose flour	675 ml (2¾ cups)	850 ml (3½ cups)	1125 ml (4½ cups)
Ground mixed spice	1½ teaspoons	2 teaspoons	2½ teaspoons
Light brown sugar	425 ml (1¾ cups)	550 ml (2¼ cups)	750 ml (3 cups)
Butter or margarine, softened	275 ml (1⅛ cups)	375 ml (1½ cups)	425 ml (1⅞ cups)
Eggs	4	5	6
Cooking times	2½–2¾ hours	2¾–3 hours	3–3¼ hours

MARZIPAN

Homemade marzipan has a taste of its own and can be easily made in manageable quantities. Ready-made white marzipan, however, is a perfectly acceptable alternative and is easy to handle.

Do take care not to over-knead homemade marzipan, as this encourages the oils from the ground almonds to flow and eventually seep through the iced surface, causing staining.

Use white or light coloured marzipan for cakes being iced in pastel shades or white, as the yellow variety can show through icing or cause staining. White marzipan is made using egg white only (see recipe).

Be sure to let the marzipan dry thoroughly on the cake before applying the icing. Set marzipan ensures a good cake shape during icing and prevents any moisture seeping through and staining the surface. Once the marzipan has been applied, store the cake in a warm dry room.

The chart on page 46 shows the amount of apricot glaze and marzipan required to cover different-sized cakes. Round cakes use slightly less marzipan than square, as the quantities given for both shapes suggest.

The amounts given in individual recipes allow for covering the cake and making any decorations required. If you are making your own marzipan, simply increase the basic ingredients (see page 46) in proportion, to give the quantity required. To simplify proportions, if necessary, make more and use any left over another time to make decorations; it will keep for up to 3 weeks. Ready-made marzipan is conveniently available in 250 g (8 oz) packs.

Also listed in the chart are the recommended cake board sizes for standard shaped cakes. As a general guide, the board should be 5–7 cm (2–3 inches) larger than the cake to give a balanced finish. If the design is to run over onto the board, select a larger one.

MARZIPAN

If you require a lighter coloured marzipan, use egg white only, instead of a whole egg.

250 g (8 oz) ground almonds
125 ml (½ cup) fine sugar
250 ml (1 cup) icing sugar, sifted

1 teaspoon lemon juice
few drops almond extract
1 medium egg or 1 extra large egg white

Makes 500 g (1 lb)
Preparation time: 10 minutes
Freezing: Not recommended

1. Place the almonds and sugars in a bowl and stir until evenly mixed. Make a well in the centre and add the lemon juice, almond extract and enough egg or egg white to mix to a fairly firm dough.
2. Knead on a surface dusted with icing sugar until smooth and free from cracks. Wrap in plastic wrap until required.
3. Use for covering cakes (see opposite) or making moulded decorations (see page 58).

APRICOT GLAZE

It's a good idea to make a large quantity, as it will keep in a screw-top jar in the refrigerator for up to 2 months.

500 ml (2 cups) apricot jam
3 tablespoons water

Makes 500 ml (2 cups) glaze
Preparation time: 5 minutes
Freezing: Not recommended

1. Place the jam and water in a saucepan and heat gently until the jam has melted.
2. Boil rapidly for 30 seconds, then strain through a sieve. Rub through as much of the fruit as possible and discard the skins.
3. Pour the glaze into a clean jar, seal and store in the refrigerator. Use as required.

APRICOT GLAZE, MARZIPAN AND RECOMMENDED CAKE BOARD SIZES

Square Round	□ 13 cm (5 inch) ○ 15 cm (6 inch)	□ 15 cm (6 inch) ○ 18 cm (7 inch)	□ 18 cm (7 inch) ○ 20 cm (8 inch)
Apricot Glaze	1 tablespoon	1½ tablespoons	2 tablespoons
Marzipan	350 g (12 oz)	750 g (1½ lb)	875 g (1¾ lb)
□ **Cake Board** ○ **Cake Board**	□ 18 cm (7 inch) ○ 20 cm (8 inch)	□ 20 cm (8 inch) ○ 23 cm (9 inch)	□ 23 cm (9 inch) ○ 25 cm (10 inch)

TO MARZIPAN A CAKE

1. Unwrap the cake and remove the lining paper. Roll the top of the cake with a rolling pin to flatten slightly.

2. Brush the top of the cake with apricot glaze. Sprinkle the work surface with sifted icing sugar.

3. Knead two thirds of the marzipan into a round. Roll out to a 5 mm (¼ inch) thickness the same shape as the top of the cake. Make sure the marzipan moves freely and isn't sticking to the surface.

4. Invert the cake onto the centre of the marzipan. Trim off the excess to within 1 cm (½ inch) of the cake. Using a small flexible palette knife, push the marzipan level to the side(s) of the cake.

5. Turn the cake right way up and place in the centre of the cake board. Brush the side(s) with apricot glaze.

6. Knead the marzipan trimmings together, taking care not to include any crumbs from the cake, then knead into the remaining marzipan.

7. Measure and cut a piece of string the whole length of the side of a round cake, or the length of one side of a square cake. Measure and cut another piece of string the depth of the cake.

8. Roll out the marzipan to a 5 mm (¼ inch) thickness. Cut out one side piece for a round cake and 4 pieces for a square cake, the length and width of the string. Knead the trimmings together and re-roll if necessary.

9. Carefully fit the marzipan onto the side(s) of the cake and smooth the joins with a palette knife. Leave in a warm place for at least 24 hours. Make sure it is dry and firm before applying icing.

Marzipanning the top   *Cutting the side piece*   *Marzipanning the side*

Square	☐ 20 cm (8 inch)	☐ 23 cm (9 inch)	☐ 25 cm (10 inch)
Round	○ 23 cm (9 inch)	○ 25 cm (10 inch)	○ 28 cm (11 inch)
Apricot Glaze	2½ tablespoons	3 tablespoons	3 tablespoons
Marzipan	1 kg (2 lb)	1.25 kg (2½ lb)	1.5 kg (3 lb)
☐ Cake Board	☐ 25 cm (10 inch)	☐ 28 cm (11 inch)	☐ 30 cm (12 inch)
○ Cake Board	○ 28 cm (11 inch)	○ 30 cm (12 inch)	○ 33 cm (13 inch)

ROYAL ICING

To produce a beautifully royal iced cake it is absolutely essential to make good royal icing, otherwise it is almost impossible to obtain a successful end result.

Royal icing is rather like a cold meringue mixture—light, smooth and glossy in texture. It should form a fine pointed peak when a wooden spoon is drawn slowly out of the mixture. This ensures that the icing will flow easily for piping or smoothly for flat icing, even though the consistencies are different (see below).

Everything must be clean and grease-free when making royal icing. Any little bits that get into the icing will come to the surface on a flat coat, or could cause the piping nozzles to block.

Fresh egg whites or dried albumen may be used—both produce good results. A little lemon juice helps to strengthen the albumen in fresh egg whites, but too much will make the icing short and difficult to pipe or spread. It is not necessary to use lemon juice if you are using dried albumen.

Glycerine is added to royal icing made with fresh egg whites to soften the icing a little, making it easier to cut. It is not necessary to add glycerine to icing made with dried egg albumen as it does not set as hard as fresh egg white icing.

Add the icing sugar gradually, mixing well using a wooden spoon, rather than beating during each addition, until the required consistency is reached.

Too much icing sugar added too quickly will produce a dull heavy icing, grainy in appearance. It will be difficult to work with and as it sets it will be chalky in appearance instead of sparkling. It will also be difficult to pipe, soon becoming short and breaking.

Once made, the icing must be kept covered to exclude all air and prevent the surface from setting. Use damp plastic wrap or an airtight container filled to the top with icing, to exclude any air. Covering with damp muslin is fine for short periods, but if left overnight the icing will absorb all the moisture, causing the consistency to be diluted.

Use small quantities of icing at a time. Place in a bowl and keep covered with damp muslin while working with it. If this icing becomes dry, causing hard bits, it will not have affected the whole batch.

Royal icing consistency

The consistency of royal icing varies for different uses: it should be stiff for piping, slightly softer for flat or peaked icing, and slacker for run-outs.

Piping consistency: when a wooden spoon is drawn out of the icing it should form a fine sharp point—termed as 'stiff peak'.

Flat or Peaked Icing consistency: when the spoon is drawn out of the icing it should form a fine point which curves over at the end—termed as 'soft peak'.

Run-out consistency: stiff peak to pipe the outlines; consistency of softly whipped cream to fill in the shapes.

If the icing is too stiff, add egg white or reconstituted egg albumen to make it softer; if the icing is too soft, gradually stir in more icing sugar until the required consistency has been reached.

ROYAL ICING (1)

This icing is suitable for flat or peaked icing, piping and run-outs. It can be tinted with food colouring as desired.

2 egg whites
¼ teaspoon lemon juice
500 g (1 lb) icing sugar, sifted

1 teaspoon glycerine
few drops food colouring(s) (optional)

1. Place the egg whites and lemon juice in a clean bowl. Add sufficient icing sugar to form the consistency of unwhipped cream, mixing well with a wooden spoon.
2. Continue adding and mixing small quantities of icing sugar until the desired consistency has been reached and the icing is smooth, glossy and light. Stir in the glycerine.
3. Add any food colourings at this stage, to all or part of the icing as required.
4. Allow the icing to settle before using; cover the surface with damp plastic wrap and seal well, or place in an airtight container.
5. Stir the icing before use to disperse any air bubbles, then adjust the consistency if necessary (see opposite).

Makes 500 g (1 lb)
Preparation time: 10 minutes
Freezing: Not recommended

ROYAL ICING (2)

Dried egg albumen can be used instead of fresh egg white to make royal icing. It is available from specialist shops in an instant ready-to-use form.

1 tablespoon dried egg albumen
6 tablespoons cold water

525 g (1 lb 1 oz) icing sugar, sifted
few drops food colouring(s) (optional)

1. Mix the dried egg albumen and cold water in a bowl.
2. Add enough icing sugar to give the consistency of unwhipped cream, mixing well with a wooden spoon.
3. Continue mixing in small quantities of icing sugar until the desired consistency is obtained and the icing is smooth, glossy and light. Add any food colourings at this stage, to all or part of the icing as required.
4. Cover the surface with damp plastic wrap or place in an airtight container and leave to stand for 30 minutes.
5. Stir the icing before use to disperse any air bubbles, and adjust the consistency if necessary (see opposite).

Makes 500 g (1 lb)
Preparation time: 10 minutes, plus standing time
Freezing: Not recommended

TO FLAT ICE WITH ROYAL ICING

1. Make a quantity of Royal Icing to soft peak consistency (see page 48) and cover with clean damp muslin. Place the cake on its board on a rigid surface.
2. Spread a layer of icing about 5 mm (¼ inch) thick evenly over the top of the cake. Remove the excess icing from the edge(s) of the cake with a palette knife.
3. Stand directly in front of the cake with a straight edge poised at the far side. Holding the straight edge comfortably in both hands, pull it towards you in one steady movement to smooth the top of the cake. If the surface is not satisfactory, spread more icing over the cake and repeat the movement until it is smooth.
4. Trim off the excess icing at the side(s) of the cake to neaten the top edge(s). Leave to dry for at least 4 hours in a warm dry place.
5. For a round cake, place the cake on a turntable and spread a 5 mm (¼ inch) thick layer of icing around the side. Remove excess icing from the edge. Place a side scraper on the side of the cake, resting it on the board. Pull the scraper with one hand while rotating the turntable with the other hand, to make a continuous steady movement, then carefully pull off the scraper.
6. For a square cake, keep the cake on a rigid surface and spread a 5 mm (¼ inch) thick layer of icing onto one side only. Remove excess icing from the edge. Pull a side scraper along the side in one movement. Ice the opposite side and leave to dry before icing the other sides.
7. Using a palette knife, trim the excess icing from the top edge(s) of the cake, and the corners if icing a square cake.
8. Repeat this process to build up 3 or 4 coats of thin smooth flat icing.
9. When the cake is finally dry, spread some icing around the board and draw a scraper over the surface, making the icing smooth and flat.

Smoothing the top

Removing excess icing

Smoothing the side

TO PIPE ROYAL ICING

Piping nozzles are available in a variety of shapes and sizes, but you can obtain excellent results with just a small selection. All of the designs in this section can be made if you have the following: plain writing nozzles Nos. 1, 2 and 3; small, medium and large star nozzles.

Use a parchment paper piping bag (see page 12) fitted with a straight-sided metal nozzle (without a collar). Half-fill the bag with icing; do not be tempted to fill it to the top as the fuller the bag is, the harder it is to squeeze the icing out of the nozzle. A good guide is the smaller the nozzle, the less icing you require.

Hold the piping bag comfortably with the nozzle through the first two fingers of both hands, and the thumbs applying the pressure at the top of the bag. The wrists and arms should be relaxed, just ready to guide the nozzle. Stand or sit comfortably, holding the nozzle poised just above the surface of the cake.

For piping beads, stars and whirls, the nozzle should be in an upright position. For lines, shells and coils, it should be at an angle to the cake. Press the bag gently with the thumbs so the icing flows on to the surface of the cake in the required design. Stop pressing and lift the bag firmly to break off the icing.

For fine lines, secure the line to the surface to start, then lift the nozzle to pipe; allow the icing to fall where required before breaking off.

PIPED FLOWERS
Secure 2.5 cm (1 inch) squares of waxed paper to icing nails with beads of icing. Pipe 4 or 5 petal shapes in a circle on each one, using a parchment paper piping bag, cut for a leaf design (see page 12). Pipe 2 threads of coloured icing in the centre of each flower, using a No. 1 writing nozzle. Transfer the flowers on the paper squares to a tray. When dry, peel off the paper.

FINE SUGAR PASTE

This sugar paste is exceptionally strong but can be moulded into very fine flowers or sugar pieces and dries quickly. It is not suitable for covering cakes. Liquid glucose and gum tragacanth are available from pharmacists and specialist suppliers.

2 teaspoons gelatine
5 teaspoons cold water
2 teaspoons liquid glucose
2 teaspoons shortening

500 g (1 lb) icing sugar,
sifted
1 teaspoon gum
tragacanth
1 egg white

**Makes 625 g
(1¼ lb)
Preparation time:**
10 minutes, plus
standing time
Freezing: Not
recommended

1. Place the gelatine and water in a heatproof bowl over a saucepan of hot water until melted, stirring occasionally.
2. Stir in the glucose and shortening until melted.
3. Place the icing sugar, gum tragacanth, egg white and gelatine mixture in a bowl and mix with a wooden spoon to form a soft paste.
4. Knead on a surface dusted with icing sugar until smooth and white.
5. Place in a plastic bag or wrap in plastic wrap and seal well. Leave for several hours before use.

MALLOW SUGAR PASTE

An easy-to-make-and-handle sugar paste. Pliable but not sticky, it's ideal for covering cakes and for making decorations. It will keep for up to 3 months.

1 envelope gelatine
3 tablespoons water
3 tablespoons liquid
glucose
1 tablespoon glycerine

few drops vanilla or
almond extract
(optional)
750 g (1½ lb) icing sugar,
sifted

**Makes 875 g
(1¾ lb)
Preparation time:**
10 minutes
Freezing: Not
recommended

1. Place the gelatine and water in a heatproof bowl over a saucepan of hot water until dissolved; stir occasionally.
2. Add the glucose and glycerine and stir until warm. Remove bowl from heat and stir in the extract, if using.
3. Stir in the icing sugar, using a wooden spoon. As the mixture begins to bind together, knead into a ball.
4. Knead on a surface dusted with icing sugar until smooth and white, and free from cracks. Store in a plastic bag or wrap in plastic wrap until required.

MOULDING ICING

This icing is quick and easy to make. It sets firm but not brittle and is suitable for icing all types of cakes and for making decorations. It will keep for up to 3 months.

1 egg white
2 tablespoons liquid
glucose

500 g (1 lb) icing sugar,
sifted

1. Place the egg white and glucose in a bowl. Add the icing sugar and mix together with a wooden spoon.
2. Knead with the fingers until the mixture forms a ball. Knead on a surface dusted with icing sugar until smooth and free from cracks.
3. Wrap in plastic wrap or in a plastic bag until required.

Makes 500 ml (2 cups)
Preparation time: 5 minutes
Freezing: Not recommended

TO COVER A CAKE WITH MOULDING ICING OR MALLOW SUGAR PASTE

1. Place the marzipanned cake on a turntable and brush lightly with sherry.
2. Roll out the icing on a surface sprinkled with icing sugar to a round or square 5 cm (2 inches) larger than the top of the cake.
3. Using a rolling pin to lift and support, lay the icing carefully over the top of the cake.
4. Smooth the icing over the top and down the side(s) of the cake with well-corn starched hands, so that the excess icing is at the base.
5. Trim off the excess icing and, with well-corn starched hands, rub the surface in circular movements to make the icing smooth and glossy.
6. Knead the trimmings together and seal in plastic wrap or a plastic bag. Use for decorations.

NOTE: After storing, sugar paste and moulding icing may become rather dry and difficult to handle. Simply knead in a few drops of water, working the icing or paste until smooth.

Positioning the icing

Smoothing the icing

Trimming off excess

DESIGNING THE CAKE

Think carefully about the celebration cake as a whole even before you make it: consider the occasion, shape, size, colour scheme and design, as well as the time involved. Choose a simple design, using simple shapes and piped work, to start with, and progress to more complicated designs as your skills improve.

Most designs need to be drawn carefully to scale and a template made to mark the design on the cake. This ensures that the design will be accurate when piped and that the cake will look good from every angle.

USING A TEMPLATE
1. Carefully measure the top of the cake and cut out a matching shape in waxed paper—it should fit the top of the cake perfectly.
2. Measure the side(s) of the cake and cut out a strip of waxed paper the exact height and length. This should fit one side of a square cake, or the whole side of a round, heart-shaped or horseshoe cake.
3. Use these pieces to make templates for the chosen design.
4. Ensure the surface of the iced cake is completely dry, then place the top template on the cake and hold in position carefully.
5. Using a pin, carefully prick around the template to transfer the outline of the design clearly onto the iced surface. Prick more detailed design through the template.
6. Place the side template against the side of the iced cake, resting on the board at the base, and mark the design as above.

TEMPLATE FOR COMING OF AGE CAKE
1. Cut out an 18 cm (7 inch) square of waxed paper.
2. Fold the square diagonally in half, then in half twice more, making a triangular shape.
3. Bring the points at the open edge to meet and fold. Place an egg cup on this open edge and draw a semi-circle. Cut carefully along the marked line.
4. Open out the template, position on top of the iced cake and prick around the design with a pin as described above.
5. Re-fold the template to form a triangle with 2 scallops on the open edge. With the edge at the top, outline the scallop design with a pencil onto a piece of waxed paper. Move the template down by 5 mm (¼ inch) and draw a second outline. Join the semi-circles with lines at each end. This will give the run-out pattern for the side pieces of the cake.

TEMPLATE FOR CONGRATULATIONS CAKE

1. Cut out a 15 cm (6 inch) circle of waxed paper for the top template. Fold it in half, then fold it in half 3 more times, making a thin cone shape.

2. Choose a small circular object, such as a meringue nozzle, place it on the wide end of the cone and draw a semi-circle.

3. Carefully cut out the shape following the marked line. Open out the template; it should have a scalloped edge, with 16 points.

4. Cut out a strip of waxed paper to fit the side of the cake exactly and fold it into 6 equal lengths, creasing the paper well on the folds.

5. Open up the strip of paper, place a ruler diagonally from the top to the bottom between 2 creases and draw a line. Repeat 5 more times between the remaining creases in the paper.

6. Using the folded top template as a guide, pencil in the scalloped design centring it on the drawn lines.

7. Place the opened-out top template in position and transfer the design with a pin as described opposite. Secure the side template to the cake with small beads of icing at the join, then transfer the design with a pin.

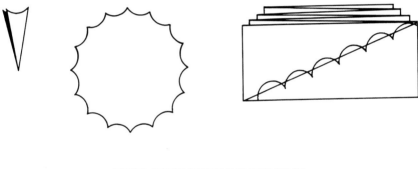

CUT-OUT DECORATIONS

Simple decorations can be cut out from moulding icing, sugar paste and marzipan, using cutters or stencils as a guide.

Alphabet cutters are particularly useful for birthday cakes etc. Holly leaf cutters are useful for Christmas decorations; mark 'veins' onto the leaves with a knife and dry over dowels or wooden handles to give a good shape.

Cut-out Flowers

1. Roll out small pieces of moulding icing or sugar paste thinly on a well-corn starched surface and cut a few shapes at a time, using flower cutters. Press the flowers into the palm of the hand to shape them.

2. Thread a stamen through the centre of each flower.

3. If required, shape the petals by pressing the centre of each one with the end of a fine paint brush to flatten.

4. Leave the flowers to dry.

NOTE: Cut-out flowers, holly leaves, letters and stars are illustrated on pages 40–1.

RUN-OUTS

Run-outs make effective decorations and they are easy to make—once you know how! They can be made in any shape or form by tracing over a chosen design or pattern and simply copying it in icing. As they are very fragile, it is wise to choose a solid shape and make more than the required amount to allow for breakages.

Begin with simple shapes, such as the bells, numerals and abstract shapes illustrated below, and allow plenty of time. As you gain confidence, try more adventurous designs. Trace outlines for robins, Father Christmas, stars, etc from Christmas cards.

Run-outs can be piped all in the same colour for the outline and the filling or, if preferred, the outline can be piped in white. They can be over-piped, or painted with food colouring when dry.

Make run-outs in advance, as they can be stored for several months.

1. Draw or trace your chosen design onto a piece of paper. Repeat the design several times, giving a number of run-outs to work on.
2. Secure the paper to a flat surface or board with tape or pins.
3. Cover each design with a piece of waxed paper or non-stick parchment paper and secure to the design paper with a few dots of icing; press down to hold firmly.

4. Make up some Royal icing (see page 49), using 2 egg whites or 2 tablespoons dried egg albumen to 500 ml (2 cups) icing sugar. Do not add glycerine or lemon juice. Transfer about a quarter of the icing to a small bowl and make sure the consistency is stiff peak for piping the outlines (see page 48). The remaining icing should be the consistency of softly whipped cream for filling in the outlined shapes.

5. Half-fill a parchment paper piping bag fitted with a No. 1 plain nozzle with stiff peak icing. Half-fill another bag with the thinner icing and snip off the point. Have a wooden cocktail stick at hand.

6. Pipe a continuous line of stiff icing around the shape to give it an outline. Fill in the shape with soft icing so that it looks over full—the icing will shrink on drying.

7. Use the cocktail stick to coax the icing to the edges of the run-out, then tap the surface or board to level the icing.

8. As each run-out is completed, place it carefully on a flat tray or board and leave in a warm place overnight or until set hard.

9. Store the run-outs on the waxed paper in an airtight container in a dry place until required.

10. Carefully peel off the waxed paper: loosen all the edges first by pulling the paper downwards, then gently pull the paper away.

MOULDED DECORATIONS

These are simply moulded from moulding icing (unless otherwise stated).
Food colourings can be kneaded in or applied to the finished decoration with a
paintbrush. Decorations should be left to dry thoroughly before use.

Sugar Roses: Colour moulding icing as desired then, using well-corn starched
hands, take a small ball of icing and press into a fine petal shape. Curl the
outside edge inwards to form a centre piece. Press out a second petal from a
small ball of icing and wrap around the centre piece, keeping it close at the base
and apart at the top. Repeat, making more petals and attaching them to the rose
until it is the required size. Cut off the stem.

Christmas Rose: Roll 7 tiny pieces of icing into balls. Using well-floured hands,
press 5 into petal shapes. Flatten another ball of icing into a round and arrange
the petals on top, then sit the flower in a cup-shaped piece of foil. Press the
remaining ball into the centre and stud with yellow stamens. Leave to set in foil,
then remove carefully.

Daffodils: Take 7 tiny balls of yellow marzipan or moulding icing. Press 6 into
petal shapes. Using the end of a fine paintbrush, press the other one to make
the trumpet shape. Assemble the petals and centre, using a little egg white.

Easter Chick: Shape a small ball of yellow marzipan or moulding icing into a
head with a beak. Shape a slightly larger ball into a body. Press out 2 tiny wing
shapes and assemble the chick, using egg white if necessary. Mark in the eyes
and beak with food colourings.

Egg Shell: Take a small ball of marzipan or moulding icing and shape into an 'egg', cut in half. Using the end of a fine paintbrush, press and hollow out the inside to form 2 shells. Shape the edges to represent a broken shell.

Christmas Bells: Mould a piece of white icing into a small bell shape and cut in half to make half bells; press into shape with the fingers. Shape 2 clappers and a bell rope. Paint on gold food colouring to finish if you wish.

Christmas Trees: Shape green marzipan or moulding icing into a cone. Using small scissors, snip at intervals working from the top down to the base and all around the cone to make a tree shape.

Snowman: Shape a head and body from moulding icing. Shape coloured icing to make a scarf, hat, nose and buttons. Paint on eyes and mouth.

Christening Bootees: Shape a small ball of blue icing into a boot. Using the end of a fine paintbrush, press to hollow out the inside. Trim with a white bow.

Bib: Press a piece of white icing into a petal shape, pressing the edge with the fingers to make it frill. Cut out the neck piece with the open end of a piping nozzle. Use blue icing for the ribbon and to decorate the bib.

Rattle: Roll a piece of white icing into a ball; wrap a thin piece of blue icing around the ball, making a small handle piece underneath. Shape a handle from blue icing and join it on.

Cover: Cut out 6 white and 6 blue, 5 mm (¼ inch) wide strips of icing, then weave together, gently pressing the strips close together. Trim to a square and place on a larger square of white icing. Brush the edges of the strips with egg white, then fold the white edges over the woven edges to neaten. Trim the corners of the cover with cut-out flowers (see page 55).

CELEBRATION CAKES

Simplicity is the essence of these beautiful celebration cakes. Most of them can be adapted to suit almost any occasion, by changing the colours or some of the piping and applied decorations.

CONGRATULATIONS CAKE

Delicately decorated, this cake will suit many occasions. The design is piped using only writing nozzles and a hint of colour added to your own choice.

23 cm (9 inch) round Rich Fruit Cake (page 42), covered with Marzipan (page 45)

2 quantities Royal Icing (page 49) food colouring

Makes one 23 cm (9 inch) round cake
Cooking time:
3¼ hours

1. Cover the top and side of the cake with several coats of royal icing, then ice the cake board (see page 50).
2. Make two templates, one for the top and one for the side of the cake (see pages 54–5). Mark the design on the top of the cake.
3. Divide the side of the cake into 6 sections, marking them with a bead of icing on the top edge. Take the side template and mark the scallops from the bead of icing diagonally to the board.
4. Using a parchment paper piping bag fitted with a No. 2 plain writing nozzle and royal icing, outline the top design, by piping a continuous thread of icing. Pipe a second thread of icing on top of the first.
5. Pipe 2 beads of icing at the point of each scallop, then pipe 3 beads of icing in between the loops.
6. Outline the design on the side of the cake in the same way, then pipe 1 bead at the point of each loop and 4 beads underneath.
7. Pipe the word 'CONGRATULATIONS' across the centre of the cake.
8. Using a No. 3 plain writing nozzle, pipe large beads of icing around the top edge and base of the cake.
9. Tint 2 tablespoons icing with a few drops of chosen food colouring. Place in a parchment paper piping bag fitted with a No. 1 plain writing nozzle and over-pipe the beads of icing and looped design.

GOOD LUCK CAKE

23 cm (9 inch) round Rich Fruit Cake mixture (page 42)	*40 piped flowers (see page 51)*
1 kg (2 lb) Marzipan (page 45)	*FINISHING TOUCHES:*
3 quantities Royal Icing (page 49)	*4 sprigs white heather*
50 ml (¼ cup) Moulding Icing (page 53)	*2 silver horseshoes*
few drops orange food colouring	*1.5 metres (1½ yards) 2.5 cm (1 inch) wide orange ribbon*
	1.5 metres (1½ yards) 5 mm (¼ inch) wide white ribbon

Makes one 25 cm (10 inch) horseshoe cake
Cooking time: 3¼ hours

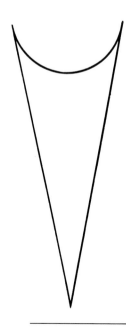

1. Prepare a 25 cm (10 inch) horseshoe-shaped cake pan (see page 41). Turn the cake mixture into the prepared pan and bake in a preheated oven, 140°C/275°F, for about 3¼ hours (see page 43).

2. Cover cake with marzipan (see page 47) and place on a 33 cm (11 inch) round or horseshoe-shaped cake board.

3. Cover the top and sides of the cake with several coats of royal icing (see page 50).

4. Colour the moulding icing pale orange with food colouring and roll out thinly. Cut out the words 'GOOD LUCK' (see page 55) and leave to dry.

5. Trace the design template (left) onto a piece of card. Place the template on top of the cake at one corner and transfer the scallop design to the cake with a pin. Move the template around the cake, transferring the design. Repeat around the top of the sides, linking the scallop points.

6. Using a parchment paper piping bag fitted with a No. 1 plain writing nozzle and royal icing, outline the marked design on the top and sides of the cake.

7. Measure 2 cm (¾ inch) up both sides of the cake from the cake board. Mark with a pin at 2.5 cm (1 inch) intervals around the outside and inside of the cake. Pipe a fine line joining these marks, to form a scallop design. Pipe 3 beads of icing where each scallop joins.

8. Tint 4 tablespoons royal icing with orange food colouring and use to over-pipe the design on the top and sides of the cake with a No. 1 plain writing nozzle.

9. Secure the flowers to the top edge of the cake in between the scallops with a little icing. Position the words 'GOOD LUCK' with the heather sprigs and horseshoes on either side, and secure with a little icing.

10. Trim the ribbons to fit around the outside edge of the cake, securing with icing.

COMING OF AGE CAKE

A versatile cake, for 'his' or 'her' 18th or 21st birthday. Run out the key and appropriate numbers in the colour of your choice, using the stencils below.

23 cm (9 inch) square Rich Fruit Cake (page 42), covered with Marzipan (page 45)
3 quantities Royal Icing (page 49)

few drops food colouring
4 run-out keys, '21' or '18', and 8 run-out side pieces (see pages 54 and 56), coloured as desired

Makes one 23 cm (9 inch) square cake
Cooking time: 3¼ hours

1. Cover the top and sides of the cake with several coats of royal icing, then ice the cake board (see page 50).
2. Make a template (see page 54) and mark the design on the cake.
3. Using white royal icing and a No. 1 plain writing nozzle, pipe a fine thread of icing following the marked design. Pipe a second thread 5 mm (¼ inch) inside the first. Fill in to make a run-out, using coloured icing.
4. Fill a parchment paper piping bag fitted with a medium star nozzle with white royal icing and pipe a coil around the top and base of the cake. Pipe a coil at each corner from the cake to the edge of the board.
5. Attach the keys, side and numeral run-outs to the cake with a little icing. Pipe beads of icing around the outside of the top design and below the side pieces.
6. Using stiff coloured icing and a No. 1 plain writing nozzle, pipe beads in between the coil edging and over-pipe those around the run-outs.

  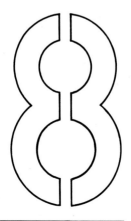

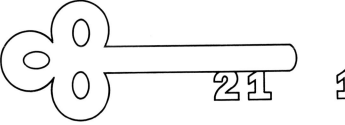

FROSTED FLOWER WEDDING CAKE

A wedding cake you can make in a few days, covered with an easy-to-make mallow sugar paste and decorated with sugar-frosted flowers and ribbons.

*1 each 25 and 18 cm (10
    and 7 inch) round Rich
    Fruit Cakes (page 42),
    covered with Marzipan
    (page 45)
2 quantities Mallow Sugar
    Paste (page 52)
1 egg white, lightly beaten
1 tablespoon Royal Icing
    (page 49)
about 90 assorted small
    frosted flowers (see page
    10)*

*FINISHING TOUCHES:
3½ metres (4 yards) 1 cm
    (½ inch) wide white
    ribbon
3½ metres (4 yards) 5 mm
    (¼ inch) wide coloured
    matching ribbon
1 metre (1 yard) each
    2.5 mm (⅛ inch) wide
    white and coloured
    ribbon
3 × 6 cm (2½ inch) white
    round cake pillars
fresh flower arrangement
    in tiny vase*

**Makes one 2-tier
round cake
Cooking time:**
3¼ hours

1. Cover the cakes with mallow sugar paste (see page 53).
2. Knead the trimmings together, roll out thinly and cut into 7 strips, each 20 × 1 cm (8 × ½ inches). Cover 3 strips with plastic wrap.
3. Place one strip on a work surface well sprinkled with corn starch. Using the handle of a fine paintbrush, firmly roll backwards and forwards until the edge of the icing is very thin and begins to frill at the edge.
4. Brush the base edge of the large cake and the cake board with a fine line of egg white. Place the icing frill around the cake, fixing it carefully to the cake and to the board. Trim ends straight.
5. Repeat with 3 more icing strips and trim to fit, so that the frill goes all around the cake and covers the board. Leave in a warm place to harden.
6. Using the 3 remaining icing strips, repeat steps 3, 4 and 5 on the smaller cake board.
7. Measure and cut the 1 cm (½ inch) wide white ribbon to fit around the base and top edge of both cakes. Secure with a little icing. Repeat with the 5 mm (¼ inch) wide coloured ribbon, positioning it on top of the white ribbon.
8. Tie 9 bows from each piece of 2.5 mm (⅛ inch) wide ribbon.
9. Arrange 5 double bows evenly around the base of the large cake, and 4 on the small cake; secure with icing.

10. Fill a parchment paper piping bag with the royal icing and snip off the point. Pipe a diagonal row of large beads on the top and side of the large cake, centred between two bows, and arrange a spray of frosted flowers on each. Repeat this design 4 more times on the large cake.

11. Repeat on the small cake, making 4 sprays. Arrange the cake pillars on the large cake and carefully position the small cake on top. Place the flower arrangement on top.

SQUARE WEDDING CAKE

This cake may look difficult, but it is very simple to make. The pretty edging and flowers are simply made with fine sugar paste and cutters, and can be done in advance. Position this cake on a 33 cm (13 inch) square cake board.

25 cm (10 inch) square Rich Fruit Cake (page 42), covered with Marzipan (page 45)
3 quantities Royal Icing (page 49)
1 quantity Fine Sugar Paste (page 52)
few drops peach food colouring

FINISHING TOUCHES:
1½ metres (1½ yards) 1 cm (½ inch) wide peach ribbon
3 metres (3 yards) 5 mm (¼ inch) wide white ribbon
1 metre (1 yard) 2.5 mm (⅛ inch) wide peach ribbon
4 tiny silver horseshoes

Makes one 25 cm (10 inch) square cake
Cooking time: 3½ hours

Fig i

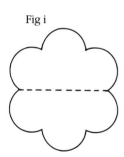

Fig ii

Fig iii

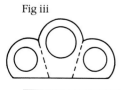

1. Cover the top and sides of the cake with several coats of royal icing (see page 50).
2. Roll out a small piece of the sugar paste on a surface well-sprinkled with corn starch. Using a 3.5 cm (1½ inch) flower biscuit cutter, cut out pieces, then cut each one in half (Fig. i). Using a 5 mm (¼ inch) and a 1 cm (½ inch) plain nozzle, cut out one large round in the centre and a smaller round at each side; discard these cut-out rounds (Fig. ii). Repeat to make 60 sugar pieces; this allows for breakages. Make the corner pieces by cutting the centre pieces from 8 sugar pieces (Fig. iii). Leave to dry.
3. Colour the remaining sugar paste peach and use to cut out assorted flowers (see page 55).
4. Using a parchment paper piping bag fitted with a No. 3 plain writing nozzle and royal icing, pipe a line along one top edge of the cake. Position the cut-out sugar pieces carefully on top. Repeat along the other edges.
5. Pipe a line of icing onto one side of the cake board at the base of the cake and secure sugar pieces onto the board. Repeat on the other sides.
6. Place 4 sugar pieces in a square on the centre of the cake and secure each with a line of icing.
7. Measure and fit the 1 cm (½ inch) peach ribbon all around the cake, securing with icing.
8. Cut 4 pieces of white ribbon to fit along the top edges of the cake. Pipe a bead of icing on each corner sugar piece. Place the ribbon along the edges of the sugar pieces; attach to the icing beads. Repeat around the base.

9. Make 8 tiny bows from the thin peach ribbon and secure with a little icing to all corners of the cake. Place a silver horseshoe at each top corner.

10. Arrange sugar flowers in the centre and at the corners of the cake, securing with a little icing.

CHRISTENING CAKE

This pretty Christening cake is suitable for a boy or a girl—simply colour the icing blue or pink. The decorations can be made in advance and stored in a container.

18 cm (7 inch) square Rich Fruit Cake (page 42), covered with Marzipan (page 45)

1 quantity Mallow Sugar Paste (page 52) food colouring 3 tablespoons Royal Icing (page 49)

Makes one 18 cm (7 inch) square cake
Cooking time:
2¼ hours

1. Cover the cake with the mallow sugar paste (see page 53).
2. Knead the sugar paste trimmings together and colour three quarters with a few drops of chosen food colouring. Use the white trimmings and a quarter of the coloured to mould the cover, bootees, rattle and bib (see page 59) and to make 16 small and 16 medium cut-out flowers (see page 55). Leave to dry.
3. Place 2 tablespoons of the royal icing in a parchment paper piping bag fitted with a large star nozzle. Colour the remaining royal icing the same colour as the sugar paste and place in a parchment paper piping bag fitted with a No. 2 plain writing nozzle.
4. Roll and trim the remaining coloured sugar paste to a strip 30 × 5 cm (12 × 2 inches). Cut out eight 5 mm (¼ inch) strips and cover with plastic wrap.
5. Pipe a dot of coloured royal icing on the top of each corner of the cake. Carefully loop a strip of coloured sugar paste on each side of the cake, pressing gently to secure at the top corners. Trim the strips neatly to fit.
6. Take one remaining strip at a time and fold into 2 loops near the centre to form a bow. Attach to the top corners of the cake with a bead of icing. Trim the ends of the pieces to the same length.
7. Pipe a bead of coloured icing on each bow and secure a medium-sized flower to each. Pipe a bead of icing into each flower.
8. Repeat to secure 3 medium and 2 small flowers on the coloured icing strip on each side of the cake, and one small flower on the board at each corner of the cake and the cover.
9. Pipe a row of white stars around the base of the cake. Pipe a bead of coloured icing on top of each star.
10. Arrange the cover, bootees, rattle and bib on top of the cake, securing each with a little icing.

SILVER WEDDING CAKE

The flowers and piped sugar pieces can be made in advance and stored in a container. You will need a 25 cm (10 inch) round silver cake board for this cake.

20 cm (8 inch) round Rich Fruit Cake mixture (page 42)
750 g (1½ lb) Marzipan (page 45)
2 tablespoons Apricot Glaze (page 46)
1 quantity Mallow Sugar Paste (page 52)
pink food colouring
½ quantity Royal Icing (page 49)

FINISHING TOUCHES:
5 silver rose leaves
silver dragees
1 metre (1 yard) 1 cm (½ inch) wide white ribbon
1 metre (1 yard) 5 mm (¼ inch) wide silver ribbon
'25' silver emblem

Makes one 20 cm (8 inch) heart-shaped cake
Cooking time: 2¼ hours

1. Prepare a 20 cm (8 inch) heart-shaped cake pan (see page 41).
2. Turn the cake mixture into the prepared pan and bake in a preheated oven, 140°C/275°F, for about 2¼ hours (see page 42).
3. Cover the cake with marzipan (see page 47).
4. Cover the cake with mallow sugar paste (see page 53).
5. Knead the trimmings together and tint pale pink with 1 or 2 drops of pink food colouring. Use to make 18 moulded sugar roses (see page 58).
6. Make 30 piped sugar pieces; this allows for breakages. Trace the outline (see left) several times onto a piece of paper and fix onto a board with tape. Secure a sheet of waxed paper over the tracings with a few beads of icing. Using a parchment paper piping bag fitted with a No. 1 plain writing nozzle, pipe royal icing in a thread following each outline. Transfer the waxed paper to a tray. Repeat to give 30 designs. Carefully peel off the paper when dry.
7. Arrange the flowers and silver leaves on top of the cake, then secure with a little icing. Attach the sugar pieces around the top edge of the cake with a silver dragee in between; secure both with a little icing.
8. Using a parchment paper piping bag fitted with a star nozzle, pipe royal icing stars around the base of the cake and top alternate stars with a dragee.
9. Trim and fit the white ribbon around the side of the cake, then place the silver ribbon on top, securing with icing. Place the '25' on top of the cake.

VARIATION

Omit the piped sugar pieces. Use the royal icing to pipe a
star edging around the top of the cake and, as for the base,
top alternate stars with a dragee.

SIMNEL CAKE

500 ml (2 cups) all-purpose flour	*350 g (12 oz) Marzipan (page 45)*
½ teaspoon baking powder	*TO DECORATE:*
1 teaspoon ground mixed spice	*1 tablespoon Apricot Glaze (page 46)*
250 ml (1 cup) light brown soft sugar	*½ quantity Glacé Icing (page 16)*
175 ml (¾ cup) soft margarine	*6 marzipan daffodils, 2 half egg shells, and*
2 teaspoons grated orange peel	*1 chick (see pages 58–9)*
1 tablespoon orange juice	*FINISHING TOUCH:*
3 eggs	*1 metre (1 yard) 3.5 cm*
350 g (12 oz) mixed dried fruit	*(1½ inch) wide yellow ribbon*

Makes one 18 cm (7 inch) round cake
Preparation time: 30 minutes
Cooking time: 1½–1¾ hours

1. Prepare a deep 18 cm (7 inch) round cake pan (see page 41).
2. Sift the flour, baking powder and mixed spice into a mixing bowl, then add the sugar, margarine, orange peel and juice, and eggs.
3. Mix together with a wooden spoon, then beat well for 2–3 minutes; alternatively, beat for 1–2 minutes in an electric mixer. Stir in the fruit.
4. Place half of the mixture in the prepared pan and level the top.
5. Roll out half of the marzipan thinly to an 18 cm (7 inch) round and place on top of the cake mixture in the pan.
6. Spread the remaining cake mixture over the marzipan and level the top with the back of a metal spoon.
7. Bake in a preheated oven, 170°C/325°F, for 1½–1¾ hours, until risen, golden brown and firm to the touch in the centre. Leave to cool in the pan, then turn out and remove the paper.
8. Brush the top of the cake with apricot glaze.
9. Cut the remaining marzipan in half and roll into 2 pencil-thin lengths. Twist into a rope and place around the top edge of the cake; trim to fit.
10. Cover the centre of the cake with foil and place under a preheated broiler until the marzipan is golden brown. Remove the foil and leave to cool.
11. Pour the glacé icing over the centre of the cake and spread carefully to the marzipan rope. Leave to set.
12. Arrange the daffodils, shells and chick on top of the cake and tie the ribbon around the side.

CHRISTMAS BELL CAKE

To save time at Christmas, make the bell shapes and holly leaves well in advance.

20 cm (8 inch) round Rich Fruit Cake (page 42), covered with Marzipan (page 45)
1½ quantities Royal Icing (page 49)

½ quantity Moulding Icing (page 53)
green, red and gold food colourings
FINISHING TOUCH:
1 metre (1 yard) each 2.5 mm (⅛ inch) wide green and red ribbon

Makes one 20 cm (8 inch) round cake
Cooking time: 2¼ hours

Illustrated bottom right: Christmas Rose Solo Cake (see page 78)

1. Ice the top of the cake only, with 2 or 3 coats of royal icing (see page 50). Leave to dry. Adjust the remaining icing to make it stiff peak (see page 48).
2. Place the cake on a turntable and spread the side with stiff icing to coat evenly, then smooth roughly with a side scraper. Remove any excess icing from the top edge.
3. Dip a small palette knife into the stiff icing and, starting at the base of the cake, press the knife onto the icing, then pull sharply away to form a peak. Continue all around the base and up to the top edge of the cake, leaving a smooth band around the middle for the ribbons. Reserve the remaining icing.
4. Colour one third of the moulding icing green and a small piece red. Cut out 12 holly leaves from the green moulding icing (see page 55) and shape 15 tiny berries from the red moulding icing. Use the remaining white moulding icing to make bell shapes, rope and clappers (see page 59). Leave to dry.
5. Brush the holly leaves with green food colouring to give a deeper shade of green, and paint the bell shapes, rope and clappers with gold colouring.
6. Place 1 tablespoon of the reserved royal icing in a parchment paper piping bag fitted with a No. 2 plain writing nozzle and pipe an edging of beads around the top of the cake.
7. Colour a little of the reserved royal icing green and some red and place each in a parchment paper piping bag fitted with a No. 1 fine writing nozzle.
8. Pipe a bead of green icing on each alternate white bead. Pipe red beads on the remaining white beads.
9. Arrange the bells, rope, clappers, holly leaves and berries on top of the cake and secure with a little white royal icing.

10. Using the white royal icing, pipe the words 'MERRY
CHRISTMAS' beside the bell rope on top of the cake, then
over-pipe, using the red icing.
11. Tie both pieces of ribbon together around the side,
making a pretty bow, and trim the ends.

SOLO CHRISTMAS CAKES

These super little cakes are made from just one 20 cm (8 inch) square cake. For maximum effect, they have been made with a variety of icings, decorations and designs. Place them on 15 cm (6 inch) square silver cake boards.

20 cm (8 inch) square Rich Fruit Cake (page 42)	*1 quantity Royal Icing (page 49)*
1 kg (2½ lb) Marzipan (page 45)	*1 quantity Moulding Icing (page 53)*
green, red and silver food colourings	*FINISHING TOUCHES:*
5–6 tablespoons Apricot Glaze (page 46)	*2 metres (2 yards) 2 cm (¾ inch) wide red ribbon*
125 g (4 oz) assorted glacé fruits	*silver and red dragees*
4 brazil nuts	*1 metre (1 yard) 5 mm (¼ inch) wide silver ribbon*
	1 red birthday candle

Makes four 5 cm (4 inch) square cakes
Cooking time: 3¼ hours

Christmas Rose Solo Cake illustrated on page 77

1. When the cake is completely cold, cut into quarters, to give 4 small cakes. Cover three with three quarters of the marzipan (see page 47) and place on cake boards.
2. Colour three quarters of remaining marzipan green. Roll out and trim to a strip, 40 × 6 cm (16 × 2½ inches). Brush the top and sides of the remaining cake with glaze and fit the marzipan strip around the side. Flute the top edge with the fingers. Place on a cake board. Arrange the glacé fruits and brazils on top and brush with more glaze. Tie 2 bands of red ribbon around the cake.
3. Flat ice one cake and the board with royal icing (see page 50).
4. Rough ice another cake (see page 76, step 3), leaving a smooth patch on the top.
5. Cover the remaining cake with moulding icing (see page 53). Knead the trimmings together.
6. Shape a snowman and 3 fir trees from the moulding icing (see page 59). Arrange them on the rough iced cake.
7. Using moulding icing, shape a Christmas rose (see page 58) and cut out 21 holly leaves (see page 55). Pipe a shell edging around the top and base of the flat-iced cake and arrange the Christmas rose and 5 holly leaves on top.
8. Colour a little royal icing red and some green and place each in a parchment paper piping bag fitted with a No. 1 plain writing nozzle. Fill another bag with white royal icing and fit a No. 2 plain writing nozzle.
9. Fix 4 holly leaves on each side of the cake. Pipe white lines between each leaf and 3 dots at one end of each leaf

to represent stems and berries. Over-pipe the lines with green icing and the dots with red icing.

10. Pipe a white dot beside each holly leaf on top of the cake and over-pipe with red.

11. For the remaining cake, cut out stars from white moulding icing: Using a medium star cutter, cut out 11 stars. Then, using a small star cutter, cut out the centres of 7 of these to make star frames. Place 4 of the tiny cut-out stars in the centre of the remaining 4 medium stars to give 4 double stars. Brush one side of each star shape with silver colouring. (Illustrated on page 40.)

12. Secure double stars to the top corners of the cake, and star frames at the bottom corners, with a little icing. Join the remaining 3 star frames together with a little icing and place in the centre of the cake with a silver dragee at each point.

13. Pipe royal icing stars a little apart around the top edge and base of the cake and place red and silver dragees alternately on these.

14. Fit the red ribbon round the side of cake, securing with a little icing, and tie the silver ribbon on top. Place the candle in the centre.

INDEX

Apple and marron gâteau 38
Apricot glaze 46

Butter icing 16

Cake pans to prepare 41
Caramel frosting 17
Chocolate:
    to melt chocolate 8
    Chocolate butter icing 16
    Chocolate crème au beurre 17
    Chocolate curls 8
    Chocolate cut-outs 9
    Chocolate decorations 8–9
    Chocolate frosting 17
    Chocolate fruit cups 20
    Chocolate fudge cake 24
    Chocolate fudge icing 16
    Chocolate glacé icing 16
    Chocolate leaf gâteau 34
    Chocolate leaves 9
    Chocolate quick-mix cake 14
    Chocolate whisked sponge 15
    Lemon and chocolate battenburg 28
Christening cake 70
Christmas bell cake 76
Christmas cakes, individual 78
Citrus crème au beurre 17
Citrus glacé icing 16
Citrus quick-mix cake 14
Citrus sponge cake 29
Citrus whisked sponge 15
Coffee:
    Coffee butter icing 16
    Coffee crème au beurre 17
Coffee frosted ring 24
Coffee frosting 17
Coffee glacé icing 16
Coffee quick-mix cake 14
Coffee whisked sponge 15
Praline coffee gâteau 32
Colours and tints 11
Coming of age cake 64
Congratulations cake 60
Crème au beurre 17
Cut-out decorations 55: in chocolate 9

Designing the cake 54–5

Equipment 6, 40

Flowers:
    Cut-out flowers 55
    Frosted flower wedding cake 66
    Piped flowers 51
    Sugar-frosted flowers 10
Frosted flower wedding cake 66
Frosting, quick 17
Fruit cake, light 44
Fruit cake, rich 42–3
Fruit frosting 17
Fruit glacé icing 16

Glacé icing 16
Good luck cake 62

Harlequin slices 19
Hazelnut strawberry gâteau 36

Leaves (chocolate) 9
Lemon and chocolate battenburg 28
Lemon rings 18

Light fruit cake 44
Lime cheese gâteau 30

Madeleines 21
Mallow sugar paste 52–3
Marzipan 45, 46; to cover a cake with 47
Minstrel boxes 18
Moulded decorations 58–9
Moulding icing 53

Orange boats 23

Parchment paper piping bag, to make 12
Pastel fondants 22
Piping, piping bags 12–13
Piping royal icing 50–1
Praline coffee gâteau 32

Quick-mix cake 14

Raspberry jelly roll 26
Rich fruit cake 42–3
Royal icing 48–9; to use 50–1
Run-outs 56–7

Silver wedding cake 72
Simnel cake 74
Solo Christmas cakes 78
Square wedding cake 68
Strawberry gâteau, hazelnut 36
Sugar-frosted flowers 10
Sugar pastes 52

Templates 54–5

Vanilla cake 27

Wedding cake (square) 68
Whisked sponge 15

Photography by: Charlie Stebbings
Designed by: Sue Storey
Home economist: Janice Murfitt
Stylist: Victoria Whately
Illustration by: Linda Smith
Typeset by Rowland Phototypesetting Limited